WRITER to WRITER

Also by Gail Carson Levine:

Dave at Night

Ella Enchanted

Ever

Fairest

A Tale of Two Castles

The Two Princesses of Bamarre

The Wish

THE PRINCESS TALES

The Fairy's Return and Other Princess Tales

The Fairy's Mistake

The Princess Test

Princess Sonora and the Long Sleep

Cinderellis and the Glass Hill

For Biddle's Sake

The Fairy's Return

Betsy Red Hoodie

Betsy Who Cried Wolf

Forgive Me, I Meant to Do It: False Apology Poems

Writing Magic: Creating Stories That Fly

Fairies and the Quest for Never Land

Fairy Dust and the Quest for the Egg

Fairy Haven and the Quest for the Wand

To you, the writers who read my blog, who share your questions and ideas, who explore with me and with each other the intricacies of writing stories and poems. How grateful I am to have your company!

Thanks to all on the blog who charged in with suggestions for the subtitle of this book. Extra-special thanks to Erica Eliza Smith for coming up with the actual, perfect subtitle!

CONTENTS

WRITER to WRITER

From Think to Ink

GAIL CARSON LEVINE

HARPER
An Imprint of HarperCollinsPublishers

Some material in this book was previously published in a slightly different form on www.gailcarsonlevine.blogspot.com.

Writer to Writer: From Think to Ink

www.harpercollinschildrens.com

Library of Congress Cataloging-in-Publication Data
Levine, Gail Carson.
Writer to writer : from think to ink / Gail Carson Levine.
pages cm
Summary: "In this lively nonfiction book for young readers, bestselling author Gail Carson Levine shares her secrets of great writing"— Provided by publisher.
ISBN 978-0-06-227530-1 (hardback) — ISBN 978-0-06-227529-5 (pbk.)
1. Authorship—Juvenile literature. 2. Creative writing—Juvenile literature. I. Title.
PN159.L48 2014 2014005858
808.02 —dc23 CIP
AC

Typography by Rachel Zegar

14 15 16 17 18 CG/RRDH 10 9 8 7 6 5 4 3 2 1

First Edition

· SECTION ONE ·

Being a Writer

SECTION FIVE: *Aspects of Story*

SECTION SIX: *Underpinnings*

SECTION SEVEN: *Poetry Country*

SECTION EIGHT: *Closing the Circle*

· CHAPTER 1 ·

Writers' Advice Column

In 2009 I started a new adventure, creating a blog—short essays, really—which I'd never done before. That I could do it is proof that if you write one kind of thing, you have a leg up on writing another. When I began, I didn't know what I'd talk about. This is from the first paragraph of my first post:

"Fear of the blank blog is as bad as fear of the blank page. For my blogging life, I intend to post once a week, and I will probably blog about writing, but I don't know that for sure. I'll see how it shapes up. If you are reading this, I would welcome a post to tell me what you're interested in reading from me."

And people did. You'll meet some of them here; their names are more various than in any baby-naming book. The blog became a writers' advice column, as you can see for yourself if you care to go online:

www.gailcarsonlevine.blogspot.com.

From early days to today, readers posted questions and I posted responses that reflect my approach to writing. A discussion of the topic followed my answer as readers added comments and more questions. Soon I noticed that I was getting even deeper into the how-to of writing than I had in my first book on writing, *Writing Magic*, and I thought, *There's a book here.*

Except for the chapters on poetry, which I added because I love to read and write poems and to teach poetry writing to kids, this book is the blog's greatest hits, according to me, rearranged and sometimes expanded. I've loved hearing from other writers—some experienced, some beginners. If you're reading this book and you've chimed in on the blog, thank you! I've especially enjoyed the mutual support in your replies to each other.

Soon after this book is published, the blog will celebrate its sixth birthday. When I assembled all my posts, the result was over 450 single-spaced pages, more than twice as long as any of my novels. There's a lot to say about writing stories.

A lot, because people tell stories constantly. We are forever shaping what happens to us into anecdotes and sometimes into grand sagas. If we can tell a good spoken story, we cast a spell over our listeners, who forget where they are and the people they're with. Instead, they picture the characters, real or imaginary, who populate our story. Our audience may be in our bedroom or on a busy street, but the scenery recedes and is replaced by the setting of our tale, which may just be somebody else's bedroom or a different busy street, or it may be an island in the middle of a stormy sea or a castle clinging to the side of a mountain.

When we write the story down, we weave the magic tighter. The more powerful our writing, the more fully we'll bring a reader into our wizardry. That's what this book is for—to make the enchantment binding.

With a little help from Shakespeare's witches in *Macbeth*, I wrote a writers' spell poem:

Mutter, mutter, dream and ponder;
Writer writes and fingers flutter.
Starting words of a startling tale,
On the paper, laugh or wail,
Days of joy and weeks of woe,
Mountains high and vales below,
Hero's hope, villain's might,
Evil's plot, virtue bright.
With this spell of flash and thunder,
In a vision, write the wonder.

As I've been writing this book, I've made a habit of starting work by rereading this spell, and sometimes I say it out loud.

You can too! Try reading or reciting it when you begin. A quick ritual can slide you into your concentration zone.

In a moment we're going to begin to write, but first, a few words about the writing prompts in these pages. They're just jumping-off points; don't feel you have to be faithful to them. You can change as much as you like: the names of the characters, the setting, the action—anything.

Whatever you write from my prompts belongs entirely to you. If an editor should want to publish a story you wrote based on one, you don't need my permission to go ahead. Naturally I'd like to hear about your triumph on my blog or my website, and I will be mighty proud of you.

Now, let's do it. Writing time! Try these:

- Pick an object in your house—could be the stove, your violin, your grandmother's running shoes, a parent's computer. Anything! Separate it in your mind from its real history and invent a history for it. Think of the drama, the tragedy, the comedy that went into its creation, its passage from owner to owner, its effect on their lives and maybe even their deaths. Write the history as a story.
- Pick a different object, which can be from your house again or your yard or the supermarket—anywhere!—and move it in your mind to a far-off location: a desert, the

bottom of the ocean, the surface of an as-yet-undiscovered planet, the cellar of a castle in a fantasy kingdom. Write a story about how it got there and how it was discovered or rediscovered.

- Give either object a magical property and write a story about how it became magical, who knows about the magic, what purposes its magic can serve. Invent characters who need the object for their virtuous or nefarious purposes.

Have fun, and save what you write, whatever you write!

Almost every chapter in this book ends with these two commands: Have fun, and save what you write! I have reasons for issuing them.

Let's start with the first command. Writing isn't always pleasurable, even for people who love to write. Sometimes ideas flee to another galaxy and won't come back. Sometimes the perfect words evaporate. *Have fun* is a reminder of why we write: to explore ideas, to follow a story, to find out what our characters will do, to entertain ourselves and our readers. The fate of planet Earth doesn't hang in the balance. We can loosen up, relax, even *have fun*.

Save what you write is important! When you save your work, you show yourself that you respect and value your efforts, even if you hate what you just wrote, even if it embarrasses you.

Keeping your writing means you're building a body of work. Story fragments are a resource you can mine. Finished stories are trophies. You can look back at them—and at your unfinished attempts—to chart your progress. Don't rip up your pages or turn them into a bonfire or hit *delete*! The consequence, sooner or later, will be regret. Pity your future biographers, who will pore over your every phrase and write dissertations on the scene you saved even though you cut it from your third novel.

Remember this about saving if you write on a computer: your writing should also be backed up somewhere, in case the computer crashes. You can't save it if you lose it.

Those are the commands. These are the rules. They appeared in *Writing Magic*, and they still apply. Here they are again:

1. The best way to write better is to write more.
2. The best way to write better is to write more.
3. The best way to write better is to write more.
4. The best way to write more is to write whenever you have five minutes and wherever you find a chair and a pen and paper or your computer.
5. Read!

6. Reread! There's nothing wrong with reading a book you love over and over. When you do, the words get inside you, become part of you, in a way that words in a book you've read only once can't.
7. Save everything you write, whether you like it or not.

· CHAPTER 2 ·

The Spark

I've been asked on the blog, and also in schools and at conferences, to say what inspires me. I suspect that there's another question locked up in this one, and that is: What tips can you give me so I can find inspiration and sustenance for my writing?

My first inspiration is my childhood reading. Reading ranked just below breathing in importance when I was little. Privacy was in short supply in our cramped apartment where I shared a bedroom with my older sister, who believed I had been created to plague her. Reading gave me privacy. The books I read then made me a writer for children now; I'm not even half tempted to write stories for adults.

Today is a great time to be a young reader, because so many marvelous books for kids have been written in the last fifty years. The ones I adored were classics: *Little Women*, *Anne of Green Gables*, *Heidi*, *Bambi*, *Black Beauty*, *Peter Pan*.

I relished books about Robin Hood and King Arthur, tall tales, and, of course, fairy tales. If I liked a book, I read it over and over. Through my favorite books I absorbed plot, character, language, even grammar. The old books didn't limit their vocabulary to what a child would know. What a gift!

So that's one tip: Sample some of these books and see if they inspire you, too.

I try to give readers the kind of story I loved, and still love, which brings me to another tip: Write for yourself, the sort of stories you like to read. Don't worry about other people's taste.

And don't worry about imitating. Writers can't avoid it. On our pages we imitate life and books and movies and TV. Being a good imitator is valuable, even essential. Imitating isn't the same as plagiarizing. We shouldn't copy another writer's exact words because there's no achievement in it, since the other person has done all the work, and because plagiarism is unethical and illegal. Our writing and that of other authors is protected by copyright law. Once you write whatever you write, it's protected whether or not you publish it. The words belong to you alone. Note that copyright covers words, not ideas. For example, you can write your own story about a girl who always obeys; the idea doesn't belong to me.

I still go to fairy tales, like "Cinderella," for ideas and inspiration. My recent novel *A Tale of Two Castles* was inspired by "Puss in Boots," leaping off from the improbable role the cat plays in the fairy tale.

Think about where you get your ideas. Fairy tales, as I do? Movies? Novels? Comics or graphic novels? Use them!

In 1987, when I started to write seriously, with hopes of being published, I read many of the Newbery Award–winning books at the library. I found in them the same old-fashioned approach to storytelling that I knew from my childhood, which made me feel right at home and as if I could join in. Another inspiration. And another tip: Catch up on your Newbery books. Your library will have them.

I took writing courses, too, and met fellow writers. My favorite class was a workshop. Every week our teacher, Bunny Gabel, would read aloud three or four selections of student work that had been submitted to her the week before. After she read, the class would comment and then she would tell us her opinion. Many published writers took this course. The same writing issues (like the ones that come up on the blog and in this book) would appear in different guises week after week, so advice would be repeated. The effect was much like rereading books; I absorbed the comments from Bunny and the more experienced writers, and now their voices are in my mind when I write. I hear them ask me what my characters are thinking and feeling or whether I've written information that the reader doesn't need to know. My teachers, Bunny and others, and my classmates are another inspiration.

You may not be able to take a writers' workshop, but you may be taking English or Language Arts in school. Pay special attention to teachers' comments on your work and also on the work of other students. If you don't understand a criticism, ask questions. When you hear something that rings true, remember it. Write it down and keep it handy. Let it permeate your consciousness when you write again. Let it inspire you.

If you don't do this already, discuss books with friends. Join a book club if you can. Analyzing books and sharing opinions will open you up to new ideas and also solidify what you believe.

Research can get me going, too. For example, I've been reading a book about the history of the Jews in Spain. I'm looking for seeds that will germinate into a story. Already I've learned how important poetry was to medieval Spanish Jews and that Jews often collected taxes for the kings, which made them hated. Both suggest ways my story might go.

And life generates ideas: overheard conversations; animal behavior; people watching; an argument you take part in; stories in the newspapers, on the radio, on the TV news; a comment by a teacher or a parent; a discovery made while completing a homework assignment.

My writing friends inspire me. Every month, two writers I've known for years come over for lunch. There's no purpose. We don't critique each other's work. Sometimes we talk shop about publishing. Often our own writing comes up. Writing is rarely smooth sailing for any of us, which is a comfort and, in an odd way, an inspiration. We're all in the same boat, and if they persevere, so can I.

Cultivate the friendship of other writers. Mostly we work alone, but our fellow strivers make us feel part of a team.

Although I enjoy being with my writing friends, I relish working alone. What keeps me writing may be the internalness of the process, the communion with myself. Like reading, writing is intensely private. We're digging in the garden of our own minds, where the bulbs and seeds we've planted with our reading, our research, and our living are sprouting, sending up flowers and veggies that have been miraculously changed from their origins, with extra petals or surprising colors or flavors never tasted before.

Writing time! These are classic topics, the sort I read about as a child, the kind that never go out of style. You've seen them in books and movies and on TV. Write a story about one or more:

- A dog, cat, or any other pet who thinks in language and is separated from its owners.
- An orphan traveling to an unknown place.
- A child separated from her family by war.
- A stowaway on a ship.
- A family struggling with poverty.
- An outlaw set against an unjust society.

Have fun, and save what you write!

·CHAPTER 3·

Drops of Blood

The imaginatively named and spelled Bluekiwii wrote on the blog about the struggle that sometimes comes with writing: "I always have the problem of actually starting to write. The story I want to write blanks from my mind, and I freeze before I've even begun to write a word. Or I'll write something, realize it's rubbish, and cross it out and begin again, and I'll continue on this way through the story until I give it up halfway. Or I sit in front of the page thinking of ideas/possibilities and reject each one. Have you ever felt this way, and what have you done to get rid of this feeling in order to write? How do you start the process of writing a story? Do you outline what you are doing first? Do you plan each chapter? How do you visualize what you're trying to write before you do it? Do you make a rough sketch of what your characters are like before fleshing them out in the story?"

I love this observation, written by journalist and playwright

Gene Fowler: "Writing is easy. All you do is stare at a blank sheet of paper until drops of blood form on your forehead."

No writer I know ever ever ever says, "I sit down at my computer every morning without fail and pop out seven glorious pages. Isn't writing the merriest activity on earth?"

Before I start a new novel, I speculate (in my notes) about what I might like it to be. Often I reread fairy tales. Also, I keep a running list of ideas for future books, and I revisit that. If any of the ideas interest me, I write more notes about it—where I could take the story, what might happen. I continue with notes and trying out new ideas until something clamors to be written. Even then I'm not sure, though, and I write more notes, until a beginning emerges. Usually I have a sense of how the story should end—nothing specific, and nothing that can't change.

Then I plunge in and start writing, without an outline but with a rough idea of where I'm going, which may be entirely different from where I end up, and occasionally I lose my way for many pages. Although I don't plan each chapter, I do have an idea of a scene before I write it, and I have an internal alarm that shrills when things are getting dull and I need to shake them up or throw in a surprise.

Naturally, this is just my method. Many writers work from outlines, which may be loose or highly detailed.

When I've got three pages, I always think, *I've written*

one percent, which is ridiculous because the book may turn out to be longer or shorter than three hundred pages, and because I'm likely to write lots of pages that I'll wind up cutting.

I do *not* ask myself if what I've written so far is any good. Such thinking is prohibited. It just gets in the way. Let's work at characters, dialogue, action, setting, and expression, and leave pronouncements on quality to the critics.

But if you must be critical, here's a trick to try:

When you think you wrote something awful, write the judgment and keep going, as in:

> *Maxine and her brother Ken left the apartment to buy a carton of milk. What garbage. Who cares? The elevator didn't come for a full five minutes, so they took the stairs. What difference does that make? I should just cut it all. Maxine had told her mother she didn't want to go to the store, but here she was, on her way. The store was boring. This is boring. I should shoot Maxine.*

Maybe it will turn out that the elevator was delayed because Maxine's upstairs neighbor, the one who gives her piano lessons, had a heart attack, and he was being carried into the elevator on a stretcher. Or maybe there will be a unicorn in the store when Maxine and Ken finally get there. Or you'll find other characters who interest you more than the two of them. When you finish the story, you can delete all the mean sentences.

And here's another trick: Write without deleting or crossing out. When you don't like what went before, just hit *Enter* twice or drop down a line in your notebook and write the sentences better or differently. If you're still not satisfied, repeat. Five is the limit, however. After five rewrites you have to move on.

Along similar lines, blog reader Mya wrote, "Homework load seems to increase every year through high school, and though I badly want to write, sometimes I can't seem to find the time. So I was wondering, how do you organize your writing time? And there is also the fact that real life can drain so much energy, making you too tired to type a single word. How do you get inspired once more, and relax into the mood?"

I'm not great at organizing my writing time. I write while I eat breakfast and while I eat lunch and at night when I have my snack. That's an hour or so. And then I write in between, but I'm very distractible. If an email comes in, I look at it. If the phone rings (rarely), I pick it up. I'm not a role model.

My method is to keep track on paper of the time I spend writing. The goal is at least two and a quarter hours of writing a day, so I write down my start times and stop times.

I may write for twenty-three minutes and stop to read an email. Before I look at the email, I note the time.

Some authors set themselves a daily page goal, say five pages, or a daily word count, say a thousand words. Both are fine practices, too.

Lots of us work well with small time goals and rewards. I'll often tell myself that if I write for half an hour, I can take a break. Not too much later I demand another half hour of myself. In doing this, I'm not thinking about finishing my book, but underneath I know that if I put in enough time at my desk and write enough pages and notes and think enough, I'll get there.

In fact, worrying about finishing is a distraction. Just write.

Thousands of people compete in NaNoWriMo—National Novel Writing Month—every year. The goal is to write a certain number of words of a novel during the month of November, a short month with only thirty days, but at least it's better than February. There's a word count for adults and one for kids. Anyone who finishes wins. It's a great goad to get you going. If you can, try it. From writers who've participated, I know that it's fun, even for those who don't win. They've put something down, created a beginning they can go back to, and there's always next year.

Sometimes I don't make my time goal, but I forgive myself, because heaping coals on my head does no good.

The coals burn! And they make getting going the next day even harder.

You can invent your own goals. Some people do better with a stick and some with a carrot. If you're a carrot kind of writer, you can write stories as gifts for the birthdays of all your friends and relatives. And for your pets! Write a story for the major and minor holidays. Celebrate National Pie Day (December 1) with a story. Or Pi Day (March 14) with a story about math.

If the stick gets you going best, devise a punishment for yourself if you fail to meet your goal. Make it awful. No more pie for a year, not even on Pie Day. If you don't care about pie, make it something that does matter to you. Swear an oath like that.

When I first began writing novels, a book trained me out of needing to be in the mood. That book, *Becoming a Writer* by Dorothea Brande, was written almost a century ago. The language is old-fashioned, but the ideas aren't. Here, in my more modern words, are three exercises from the book:

- For the next week, wake up fifteen minutes to an hour early and write right away, before you've had breakfast or changed out of your jammies, and especially before you read anything, preferably before you speak to anyone. With luck, your mind will be empty of your conventional way of thinking and surprising ideas will pop up.

- For the following week, set aside a particular fifteen minutes a day for writing. No matter what may come, you have to write during that time.
- For the last week in this program, write for fifteen minutes at different, random times. The purpose of this is to accustom yourself to writing whenever possible in any circumstance and not to depend on your mood or on a particular place. If you can write only in your bedroom or only when there's absolute silence, your opportunities narrow. I write in airports, on planes and trains, in hotel rooms. In an airport, for example, under a giant TV blasting endless headlines, weather, and commercials, I can still write. I'm irritated. I wish the thing would shut up, but I soldier on.

Doesn't matter what you jot down during these periods. It can be notes, journal entries, thoughts, or stories. Whatever it is, remember: You're writing. This, too, should be saved.

Each writer works uniquely. I'm a start-and-stop writer; I'm willing to be interrupted and I interrupt myself—but I always return to my computer. You may dive in and not come up for air until someone demands your participation in family life or until you have to go somewhere. Then you may forget about writing for days. Maybe you charge ahead, but you can't stand to look at what you've written. Or you have to rewrite every sentence a dozen times before you can move forward. Or you need a deadline to shove you along, and then your pent-up inventiveness pours out.

This exercise is from me: Observe yourself as you write, as if you were a wild creature in its natural habitat. Don't change anything or bemoan anything. Marvel at yourself. Write a journal entry about you, the writer.

And here are two more exercises:

- Sometime this week, write outside your comfort zone. Write in the living room while the family is watching television. Bring your pad to breakfast and write while you chomp down on your pancakes or your high-fiber cereal. See if you can zone out the distractions, or see if the distractions themselves take you somewhere unexpected.
- Also this week, write in an unaccustomed mode. If you usually write longhand first, go directly to a computer, or vice versa. See if there's a change in your writing. Does the new method expand you? (You can then return to your usual way, but sometimes it's helpful to shake things up.)

Of the writers I know, some write at a certain time. The hour arrives, and they sit at their desks, hoping that routine will prime the muse's pump. Some free write (write whatever comes to mind) before they enter the "real" manuscript. Some edit the work of the previous day before they pen or type a new word. Some snack their way through an entire book (carrots and celery, to be sure).

The point is that mechanics, not inspiration, keeps us writing. Continuing in the face of bewilderment eventually earns us inspiration. Habit—I can't emphasize this enough—gets us through.

So here's my advice:

1. Establish writing habits, whatever they are: a particular time to write, a number of pages that have to be written, a time goal. If you choose my method, the time goal, write the time down as you go. Don't let it be vague.
2. Know that you are a writer and your obligation—possibly your calling—is to write.
3. Forgive yourself if (and probably when) you fall short.

In case you need something to write while you try all the exercises in this chapter, here are two prompts:

- Your main character (MC), Eraxo, has an awful case of writer's block and a looming deadline. Although his writing is blocked, his ingenuity isn't. In the time freed up by not writing he invents a device to slow time and give himself as long as he needs to work through his writing paralysis. He sits at his strange machine, dons the headset, turns the dials, lifts the levers, and pushes the start button. Everything works. He has slowed time. But he discovers that his surroundings change with tempo and that creatures live here who are invisible at humanity's ordinary pace, and they are not happy about being discovered. What happens?

- Eraxo's sister, Eraxa, recognizes that she lacks the writing spark, but she wants it. She loves books, and her morals are not strong. She's as clever as her brother, so she invents a time-travel machine. She will go into the future and steal a bestseller, then return to the present and submit it to a publisher as her own. However, in the future she makes a dire discovery about the fate of books and reading and publishing. When she returns to the present, she has new and unexpected choices that challenge her questionable moral fiber, her courage, and her foresight. What happens?

Have fun, and save what you write!

· SECTION TWO ·

Character Building

· CHAPTER 4 ·

The Depths

In planning this book, I organized my posts into categories. The longest category, the one I got the most questions on, was character development, and the most persistent subcategory concerned creating characters with depth.

So let's jump in at the deep end.

This came from Jaime: "I really need to learn how to make my characters more dimensional."

In my response I admitted that I'm uncertain about my characters near the beginning of a book when we haven't been together for very long. I haven't dropped them into many situations yet and seen their reactions or dreamed up reactions for them. I'm feeling my way.

When I was three years old, my mother took me to a university for an intelligence test. I'm not sure why, but I suspect I wasn't talking as fluently as my older sister had at the same age. I remember the event because my mother made me promise not to tell my father. The examiner, a friendly man, asked me what a puddle was, and I couldn't find the words to explain. I smiled at him and shrugged. Inside I felt frustrated and foolish. Of course I knew what a puddle was!

Afterward, he told my mother that he'd worried about me at the beginning but then I'd improved. He wound up concluding that I was normal. On our way home, I remember having the forgiving thought that naturally my mother needed me to take the test. I was only a few years old, and she hadn't figured me out.

At the time I was the newest character in the tale of our family. The authors of me—my parents—didn't know me well yet. My mother was trying to discover what role I'd play in our ongoing saga. So it is with our fictional families. We have to put our characters to the test of story events to find out who they are.

Suppose, for example, that a character named Patrick somehow loses the allowance money he's been saving for a year. How will he react? If I've just invented him, I don't know. I don't even know why he was saving. So I think about what his response might be, write notes and list several possibilities, pick one, and keep going. What he does about the lost money may give me a clue to how he'll behave later when he has an important exam coming up. I already know that he saved for a year, so he prepares for the future. But since his preparation did him no good, maybe he'll decide to wing the test. Or he may do something entirely different.

Again I choose, this time with the help of Patrick's previous actions. As I continue, the effect snowballs. I understand Patrick better because of the weight of his history.

The point is not to feel that you've failed if you haven't mined the depths of your characters right away. Just keep throwing them into new situations and help them find themselves. As they do, they'll become complex.

There's more coming up on developing complicated characters, but first it's writing time!

Let's get into Patrick's heart and mind by inventing new challenges for him.

- Write a scene in which Patrick finds a wallet on the street. This is after he's lost his savings, and the money in the wallet roughly equals his loss. How does he handle his ethical dilemma?
- Patrick wins the lottery and the prize is in the millions. He's greedy. Make trouble for him with his new wealth.
- Patrick's best friend, Kaylie, texts him that he's never there for her, that he's selfish and thoughtless, and

everyone agrees with her, and she doesn't want anything to do with him anymore, and he shouldn't even text her back. Jot down three possible responses from him. Pick one and write the story.

Have fun, and save what you write!

·CHAPTER 5·

Character Cogitation

So far we've gone into what Patrick might do, but actions are only one of the tools for making multidimensional characters. What else do we have?

- Thoughts.
- Feelings.
- Speech and writing. Writing includes letters, journals, text messages, and the like. Speech, naturally, is dialogue.
- Appearance.
- Setting, sometimes.

Let's start with thoughts. Remember the prompt in the last chapter about Kaylie's text message? What does Patrick think about her accusations?

He might think, *Kaylie is hysterical again. I wish she*

didn't get like that. His ruminations might continue in the vein of countercriticism.

Or he might think, *She's right. When things go wrong, I forget everything else.*

Or, *I have to change her mind! I'll give her a present. Wait, I don't have money to buy a present.* And he's back to obsessing about himself and his loss.

It's writing time: List three more thoughts that Patrick may have about Kaylie. Save them.

Notice that Patrick's thoughts help define him, just as his actions do. In the first example, because he thinks that Kaylie has overreacted, we wonder about her. If we find out or already know that Kaylie does take offense easily, we're likely to regard Patrick as accurate and in the right. But if Kaylie is calm and levelheaded, we'll form a different impression of Patrick, a negative one.

We probably like him in the second instance, because his thoughts reveal him as willing to accept a difficult home truth.

In the third case we may start agreeing with Kaylie.

Notice that I've given Patrick's thoughts in the first person. We can present thoughts and feelings only from two points of view (POVs): from Patrick himself as a first-person narrator, or from a third-person narrator who can inform the reader of the contents of Patrick's mind. If

Kaylie is telling the story, we'll discover Patrick's thoughts only if he mentions them in speech or writing.

Ways of thinking are probably as distinct as ways of speaking. I say *probably* because I can't be absolutely sure, since I'm not telepathic. It's hard even to listen in on our own thoughts; we have to split ourselves in two to do it!

Try for yourself. What happens to me, the moment I attempt it, is that the thoughts I was hoping to eavesdrop on cease and switch over to the thoughts of me endeavoring to listen. I remember what I had been thinking, but I can't quite catch myself in the act.

Still, we often guess other people's thoughts from what they say and do, from knowing them. Sometimes we get in trouble for expressing our guesses.

Patrick, as we imagine him, may cogitate in long, looping sentences with many clauses and parenthetical asides. He may doubt himself in every other thought. Or he may think in short bursts of certainty. Or any other way. His mental processes give him depth, whether he's a deep thinker or not.

The timing of a thought needs some consideration, too. Intense action—for instance, while Patrick is racing away from the bully he just accused of stealing his allowance—may not be the moment for lengthy contemplation. We can give him a quick thought or two and delay the rest until he's hidden himself in an abandoned shed.

It's possible, however, that Patrick is a compulsive thinker. Even while he's running so hard he can barely breathe, he's musing about his birthday in two weeks that he may not live to enjoy, or he's looking at the bright side: if the bully catches him and puts him in the hospital, Kaylie will pity him and forgive his bad behavior.

Or Patrick may not be introspective. He doesn't do much reflection on the page no matter how much we want him to. We're stuck with his actions, his limited thinking, and what other characters say to him about himself.

Hey! you may be thinking. *We're stuck with Patrick? But we made him up.* Yes, we're the creators, but once we invent a character and a situation, we've narrowed the future possibilities. Our story has momentum. Patrick is now destined to think certain thoughts and make certain decisions. Other thoughts and actions have become out of character, unless we go back and change him.

Time for thinking prompts!

- Imagine Kaylie's side of the friendship. She's in her room, fuming about Patrick. Write her thoughts, either from her POV or from the viewpoint of an omniscient (all-knowing) narrator.

- Here's an old nursery rhyme, which you may know:

  Little Miss Muffet
  Sat on a tuffet,
  Eating her curds and whey;
  Along came a spider,
  Who sat down beside her
  And frightened Miss Muffet away.

  Tell the story of the nursery rhyme from the spider's POV. Give it spidery thoughts, whatever they are. Make up the workings of a spider's mind.

- Estelle and Joe have been assigned a homework project together in magic school even though they hate each other. Each plans to make the other look bad. They meet at Joe's house to work on the project. As the omniscient narrator, show how it goes, dipping frequently into the thoughts of each one. Make Estelle's way of thinking different from Joe's.

Have fun, and save what you write!

·CHAPTER 6·

Fear of Flat

When my first and excellent editor, Alix Reid, would edit my manuscripts, she used to sprinkle the word *flat* here and there—at random, it seemed to me. *Flat* was the edit I most hated to see. *What's wrong with this?* I always thought and never asked. I just tried to make the flat words plumper, rounder, better. Whatever I'd written usually did get better, just because if you pay close attention to anything, you can improve it. But Alix's meaning eluded me.

In time, however, I've come to understand what she meant. A sentence like *I'm scared* would warrant a *flat*. *I'm scared* is a summary statement, not specific, not very interesting. The reader might reasonably want to know how this particular character is scared.

Along these lines, a writer who called herself F commented on the blog: "I have difficulty in 'feeling' for my characters." She added that they seem "just the little bit too flat, and too listless."

There's a reason the word *feelings* is a synonym for *emotions*—we feel our feelings in our bodies as well as in our minds. Once, when I wanted to show how a character was scared, I hunted online for new ways to reveal fright and brought up images of terrified people. I discovered that we all look a lot alike when we're scared. Although I'd hoped for more variety, these are the signs I saw: mouth open in a scream or partially open with the lips curving down, curled hands near the neck or mouth, a lot of whites of the eyes, raised eyebrows. Then I typed "fear response" in my search engine and read about fear. We all look much alike when we're afraid because the same processes are going on in the brains of all of us. Or most of us—the article didn't mention trained assassins or the insane. When terror strikes, several parts of our brains get into the act to make blood rush from our skin (so we pale) to the muscles that can fight or carry us away. Our hearts speed up; our blood pressure rises. This inner brouhaha causes the reactions I saw in the photographs.

As I learned about fear, my heart started racing, which is the effect we want to cause in our readers. When we write fear well, they're likely to be scared too.

If our POV character is Patrick again and he's afraid or in the grip of another strong emotion, he can reveal his feelings in thoughts or physical responses—and when he does, they will no longer be flat. If he's running from a bully, he can report that his legs are burning and his heart is galloping a mile ahead of his body. If Kaylie is the one who's frightened, Patrick can relate how she seems to him, that her face is pale except for two dots of pink on her cheeks, that her eyes look watery, that she's panting and her voice sounds breathy.

Notice that Patrick experiences what's happening to himself internally. He won't know he's pale unless he's looking in a mirror or unless somebody tells him. He may assume that Kaylie's heart is pounding, but he can't be sure unless she says so.

Possibly, what makes Kaylie vibrate with terror leaves Patrick unmoved. Or vice versa. And this is how emotion contributes to character development. When we find out that hearing a raised voice causes Patrick to shudder, but crossing a rope bridge over a thousand-foot chasm doesn't speed up his heart in the slightest, we know him better. We also grow more interested in him. We wonder why shouting is so frightening. Did something horrible happen to him, something that was accompanied by yelling?

Then there's the duration of a feeling, which also varies from person to person and character to character. Patrick may take an hour to calm down from an overheard shouting match, or it may trouble him for only a minute.

Let's switch from fear to anger. Some characters blow up and blow over. They explode. Then they're fine. Others cannot let go of their fury. Patrick thinks he and Kaylie are back to being best buddies. A week passes and something tiny sets her off, a misunderstanding. She realizes that it was nothing more, but the rage returns. She may want to get past it but she can't. When we discover this about her, we understand her better.

Duration applies to thoughts, too. Some characters never drop an idea. For good or ill they pursue it. Some flit from notion to notion, rarely holding on to a thought long enough to examine it.

And there's a character's resting state, the emotion he lives in, his usual mood. Patrick may be generally cheerful, fearful, trusting, suspicious, angry, calm, or anything else. Likewise Kaylie, or any of our characters.

Writing time!

- Your MC is about to travel alone for the first time. Make up the circumstances that occasion the trip. Everybody packs differently and faces a departure differently. How does your character do it? What are his or her thoughts and feelings about it? If the story grabs you, keep going.

- Elinor arrives for the second week of her training as a scout for King Aldric in his war against the cruel dwarfs of Akero. When she gets there, she's told that she's been dropped from the cadre. Write three responses from her. If you like, choose your favorite and continue the story.
- Bonnie is depressed. Action seems hopeless. Nothing will do any good. Her alarmed parents start making her wishes come true in order to cheer her up, with results that are temporary at best. Give her a problem that activates her and lifts her depression. Write the story. At the end she can be sad again, or not.

Have fun, and save what you write!

·CHAPTER 7·

Use Your Words

So far we've delved into three mainstays of character development: action, thoughts, and feelings. Now for the fourth, speech. Writer Amy G. commented on the blog, "How do you write believable dialogue that is unique to each character's personality?"

You and I have different ways of speaking. Everyone does. I use some expressions more often than others; so do you, but not the same ones. I may speak in exclamations, you in questions. I may fly from topic to topic. You may stick to the point. I may repeat myself until you want to scream. You may leave out important details. These options don't exhaust the possibilities, which are legion.

Here's an early-in-the-chapter dialogue prompt: As you go through your day, notice your own contributions to conversation, what you say, how you say it, what you repeat, what you keep to yourself. Pay attention to what causes you to speak and what shuts you up, because silence defines a character too. Later, when you're by yourself, write about what you discovered. Include any fragments of dialogue that you remember. The next day, observe the speech of others. Write about those discoveries, too. If you're inspired, use what you found out in a new story. Then save it. Save it all, whether you write a story or not.

We're talking beings. Throw a few strangers together for more than a couple of minutes and somebody is likely to speak. Let's imagine a group of campers and Marianne, the counselor instructing them in rock climbing on the first day of camp. Marianne probably feels she needs to give some directions. That's dialogue, and how she does it reflects her personality—her character. If she's kindly, she may reassure the campers. If she's severe or in a bad mood, she may scare them. Or she may think that terrifying her charges is funny. Alternatively, she may be flighty and veer off into memories of past climbing adventures instead of conveying important information. Her omissions may put everyone in danger, an example of dialogue contributing to plot.

Will, a camper, could be timid. The climbing scares him. Depending on other aspects of his character, he may reveal his fear in dialogue or pretend it doesn't exist in different dialogue or hide it in silent teeth gritting. It's up to you.

Beth, another climber, could have a series of questions for Marianne. Val can be given to putting herself down out loud, as in, "No way am I good enough to climb this cliff." Christopher may be nosy and angling for gossip about each of his companions.

There's more to dialogue than words. Perhaps Marianne speaks so softly that the campers ask her to repeat herself until they give up, which may result in disaster on the mountain. Or she shouts her words, as if everyone else is deaf.

A fifth camper, Theo, could be superfocused. He interrupts often, without thinking about it, possibly without being aware of his rudeness. He wants what he wants, and he doesn't care what anyone else has to say on the subject. Beth, who thinks she knows everything, can also interrupt—same behavior, different reason.

Their natures issue forth in dialogue.

And in writing. One camper may be blogging about the climb. Each of them may be required to write home at the end of every day. How they express themselves will tell the reader something about them. So will their text messages to friends, which may be even more revealing. And their journals can be most revealing of all.

For example, Val could boast about climbing the mountain when she writes to her parents, but when she texts her friends, she's back to self-deprecation (the self put-downs), and when she blogs, she doesn't mention herself but describes everyone else's exploits in comic detail. Her journal entry is about how much she dislikes Christopher and how bad the camp food is.

Character is exposed not only in what Val writes but also in how she writes it. She may express herself on the page exactly as she sounds in speech. Or not. Her writing can be stiff and awkward or flowing and complex or filled with slang. There's as much variety in a character's writing as in her speech. Val may have a huge vocabulary, which she hides when she speaks. We can tell the reader in narration that her handwriting is impossible to read or that it's neat and careful. She can be a terrible speller or a good one.

Writing time!

- Invite some friends over, or try this with family. Give each person a character description. Suggest a situation that's fraught with trouble and have them act it out in character. For example, your pals or your family are trapped together in the bottom of a mine. Or they have a school assignment to write together about endangered species, and half their final grade will depend on it. Or they're going against one another in some kind of competition. Don't you be one of the characters. You're the observer, writing notes, jotting down dialogue. You can stop the action whenever you want and ask a character to repeat a line that went by too fast.

- Josie wants to do something that is certain to turn out badly. Two of her friends are trying to talk her out of it. Make up the foolhardy act. Decide whether or not the friends succeed—or whether she persuades them to help her do this crazy thing. Write the scene. Turn it into a story, using the consequences of the discussion.
- Devin has just begun his apprenticeship to a magician. Write letters from him to his parents, his sister, and his best friend. Write an entry in his diary. Have him read a page in one of the magic books that the magician has written, which you need to write too. Let Devin discover a packet of letters to the magician, and show fragments of a few of them to the reader, which means you have to write them as well. In these various writings, hint at future trouble. If you like, keep going with the story.

Have fun, and save what you write!

·CHAPTER 8·

The Outward Show

They say, "You can't judge a book by its cover." But, alas, when it comes to people as well as books, we do. We pick out future friends and ignore others with no more information than looks, a tone of voice, a laugh. This is our fifth tool for character development—appearance, the outward show. I wrote about the subject after comments like this one from Fighting Irish Fan 1111, who wrote, "Any suggestions about how to approach looks, personality, and other descriptions would be great!"

We judge more than people in an instant. We judge animals, too. That cockroach may be a friendly little guy, but most of us think he's gross. And this giant panda may be cruel to his pet bunny, but we assume he's gentle and sweet.

Let's talk about me for a minute. I'm very short. I never made it to four foot eleven. My actual height is beyond my control, but I could wear high heels. I don't. I'd rather be comfortable than slightly less short. That choice says something about me. My posture does, too, I suppose. I've worked at it, and I stand pretty straight, which probably gives me an extra eighth of an inch of height. Am I obsessing? Height is important to the vertically challenged, or at least to me. What flats and good posture convey in a story may vary, depending on other aspects of the character. Or these details may be all we decide to give the reader. Not much, but in a minor character we need no more than a quick impression.

Before we even get to clothing, there are lots of ways people and characters define themselves through appearance. Here's a prompt: Write down every element of physical description you can think of. Just a list. Don't do anything with it. These are a few items to start you off:

- A slouch (bad posture).
- Bow legs.
- Small eyes.
- A tattoo or many tattoos.
- Muscular.

See if you can get a page or two in your list, a few words to a line. Add to the list whenever you think of or observe something unusual. With your list in mind, watch people over the next few days.

Notice that I included in my starter list both characteristics that have nothing to do with the personality inside the body, like small eyes, and characteristics that are based on a decision, such as a tattoo. Include both kinds in your list, which can become a resource for you whenever you write physical description.

I was riding the New York City subway not long ago. Sitting across the aisle was a woman who seemed to be looking at me beseechingly. I couldn't tell if she meant it, and I didn't know how she did it. She said nothing; she wasn't crying. But I got a sense of sadness and need. Was it the blue eye shadow and the bags under her eyes? I don't know. I do know that she sat pigeon-toed, and the turned-in toes added to the woe somehow. The eyes and the toes would go on my list.

I've discovered that if I try to describe a character strictly from my imagination, the result isn't very interesting. I typically write about size of features, eye color, hair color, whatever comes most quickly to mind. Looking at actual people is much better, but I don't like to stare, so I go to photographs and portrait art. For example, when I wrote *The Wish*, I wanted the main male character not to be either classically handsome or hideous. I went to my high school yearbook (from 1964—yikes!) and paged through it.

The possibilities astonished me. We may not want to go into all this detail in a story, but the shape of every upper lip is different, and the space between the lip and the nose is different. In some faces the width or narrowness of the chin determines the curve of the lips. In other faces, lip shape and chin shape have nothing to do with each other. For *The Wish*, I found a boy whose eyebrows met over his nose, forming a unibrow. I never knew the owner of the eyebrow (our graduating class was very big), so I have no idea whether it ruined his high school years or didn't affect them at all. I lifted it off his face and gave it to my character, and that unibrow helped pull the plot along.

For *A Tale of Two Castles*, I looked at drawings by early-sixteenth-century artist Albrecht Dürer and found a profile view of a youngish man with a plump face; uplifted eyebrows under small mounds of flesh, as if he might sprout horns; a flat nose with two bumps; small lips; several descending chins, the topmost of which stuck out almost as far as the tip of his nose. I couldn't possibly have made him up out of my imagination.

When we're creating physical description, we want to design a face and a body that go with a character. This Dürer portrait doesn't have a face I'd give to a poet. It's a shrewd face. I bet he can add a long string of dollars and cents in his mind. I suspect he can size up a person in a second. He could be a merchant or a shady character who lives by his wits. In my book he became Master Sulow, leader of the local acting troupe, who is exceedingly shrewd.

The meaning of a characteristic will vary from person to person, just as the habit of interrupting from the last chapter had a different cause for Theo and for Beth. Take Theo, who slouches. This habit may mean he feels too tall. Or his father always told him to stand straight, so, rebellious by nature, he trained himself to slouch. Or he admires an actor who slouches. You may be able to come up with three more reasons for his bad posture. Try it. Write them down and save them. Then give tattoos to Beth and invent five explanations for them. Write these down, too.

In our story about Theo we may tell the reader why he slumps, or we may not. His posture can just become one facet of the reader's idea of him. Ah, yes, the reader thinks, this character would droop. Our reader's understanding of him will grow as she amasses information, because we're using our character development tools.

Let's move along to the fascinating and mostly voluntary aspects of appearance: clothing, hair, and, for female characters primarily, makeup. Here are some questions we might ask when we're designing a particular character, and most apply to male and female characters alike:

- Does she dress (and do her hair and makeup) to draw attention to herself or to disappear?
- What do we learn about his taste from looking at him?

- Does she wear the "right" thing or the "wrong" thing? For example, does she show up for a picnic in clothes that mustn't get dirty?
- How much choice does he have? Do his parents pick out his clothes? Can the family, or he himself, not afford much in the way of fashion? Is he color blind (color blindness is more common in males)?

Write down three more questions you can ask and save them.

These are two examples of character description. The first comes from my book *The Wish* and is told from the first-person POV of MC Wilma, who adores dogs:

> *Suzanne was tiny and perfect and had a teeny voice that carried a million miles. She reminded me of a Pomeranian—fox face and needle-sharp bark, and nervous, darting brown eyes.*
>
> *Ardis, on the other hand, was tall and bigboned and regal. She was African American, with the shaggy hair of an Irish water spaniel. Her nose was hawkish, but her eyes were huge and an amazing blue-gray, and her mouth was made for lipstick ads.*

And the second is from *Go and Come Back* by Joan Abelove, which is told from the POV of a South American tribal girl. In this paragraph she's describing the arrival of two anthropologists from the United States:

> *They looked like plain old gringos to me. One was very tall and skinny, with long yellow hair. The other one looked a little more like us, nice and fat and not tall, but her skin was a funny shade of pink. Her hair was not black enough or straight enough. It was long, but she had no bangs. They both wore no beads, no nose rings, no lip plugs, no anklets. They didn't pierce their noses or their lower lips. They didn't bind their ankles or flatten their foreheads. They did nothing to make themselves beautiful.*

Wow! In this one we don't learn only about the newcomers. We also find out something about the appearance of the narrator and others in her tribe.

Now that I've described some options, let me add that we probably don't want to stop our story for a half page of description whenever a new character shows up. We can present a little bit for a first impression and drop in more as we go along. For example, in M. T. Anderson's *The Astonishing Life of Octavian Nothing, Traitor to the Nation*, Octavian's mother is first merely called a "great beauty," and a few pages later her smile is portrayed as "slow-spreading across her soft and radiant features." That's it. Her good looks interest the reader, who waits willingly—I did—for more as the story progresses.

Time to read and think and write!

- Look at a few of your favorite books and notice how each author handled introducing the appearance of the first character you come to and how detailed or sketchy this description is. Then revisit some of your own old stories. If you decide you might have been more inventive and you're in a revising mood, try a new way or more than one. Go to your list for characteristics you haven't tried before.
- This is to be done the next time you're among strangers—in a store, a park, a sports stadium, wherever. Listen to voices without looking at the speakers. Form an image. If you can, jot down a few notes. Now look.
- Leonard is at a Halloween party dressed in a spacesuit. Without removing a bit of his costume, find a way to describe him as he looks the rest of the year. Find another way. And another.
- Look at photographs and portraits, but not of models or movie stars (not of physical perfection). Find one that interests you. Describe the character that might belong to the body—or go against type and describe a

personality that seems accidentally planted there. Write a story about him or her.

- Your MC Victoria is starting a new school at the beginning of your story. She's nervous and wants to make the right impression. Depending on her personality, she may want to fit in or to surprise people or even to shock them. Describe her in her own words. Don't have her look in a mirror, because mirrors as a vehicle of physical description (and as portals to another world) are so overused that we want to stay away from them unless we can do it in a new and surprising way.

Have fun, and save what you write!

· CHAPTER 9 ·

Here We Are

Sometimes setting contributes to character development. Sometimes it doesn't. Going back to the campers in chapter 7: If they're camping in a wilderness, for example, the mountains and trees have nothing to do with their personalities, although the choice of this particular camp may. Theo could be there because he wants to beat his older brother's record as the best rock climber in camping history. Beth's reason could be that her best friend talked her into going when she really would have preferred music camp.

No matter where a story takes place, the details that characters notice will reveal their personalities. In the wilderness, Will, who's fearful, may concentrate on how sheer the climbing cliff is. Theo, who's focused, will see the hand- and toeholds. Maybe only Marianne, the counselor, will be alert to the beauty that surrounds them.

Setting reflects character the most when the character has a hand in creating it. For example, we learn something about Beth from the way she decorates her locker at school, or about Theo from the posters he puts up in his bedroom or from his bedroom itself—if he picked the furniture and the paint color.

How messy or neat is the room or the locker? If it's messy, what's in the mess? Is there an odor? Eew! If the room is neat, are we talking super neat, with every edge exactly parallel or perpendicular to every other edge? Does Theo straighten the items on his desk for fifteen minutes before he's able to go out?

In *Peter Pan* James M. Barrie describes Tinker Bell's recess in the underground home of Peter and the lost boys, including "a genuine Queen Mab" couch, a "Puss-in-Boots" mirror, "the carpet and rugs of the best (the early) period of Margery and Robin." And more. At the end—and I think this is so cool!—he sums it all up by telling the reader how the place expresses Tink's personality:

> *Her chamber, though beautiful, looked rather conceited, having the appearance of a nose permanently turned up.*

In addition to setting itself, how a character acts in a setting reveals her, too.

Let's imagine Beth in the wilderness, only this isn't the ordinary wilderness of campers and camp counselors and cell phones. Although Beth went to sleep in that place last night, this morning the forest is different. She wakes up wrapped in a scratchy wool blanket instead of her sleeping bag, and she's stiff with cold. The wind is howling. Yesterday the birds blared out their songs, but today they're silent. Beth smells smoke on the wind. Her friends are gone. Only one camper remains, Yura, whom Beth hardly knows, who said little yesterday but who scampered up the cliff as though gravity had no hold over her.

What does Beth do? Jump up and chant, "Bring it on, bring it on," then pump out a dozen perfect push-ups? Bury her face in the leaves under her nose and wait for the hallucination to pass? Scream? Sit up and peer around cautiously? Ask Yura if she knows what's going on?

Each choice says something about Beth. Let's consider the last two, the mildest reactions. Taking in the environment without speaking may mean that she's self-reliant or that she's shy, even in these circumstances. Or both. Or something else that I haven't mentioned. Speaking to Yura may mean that she depends on other people or that she's naturally outgoing. Or something else. We'll find out more as we go along. These initial reactions to a setting form an impression that influences us as we continue to write.

In more mundane surroundings people interact with place all the time. You're alone in somebody's kitchen. Maybe your friend has gone to the bathroom or to answer the door. Do you stay in your chair or get up to investigate? If you investigate, do you touch? Do you eat a cookie from the plate of snickerdoodles cooling on the windowsill? Do you gulp it down guiltily when you hear your host returning? Or do you chew openly and say how good it is? Or—you wouldn't do this!—do you say it could use more sugar?

I often ride a commuter train from my home to New York City and back again. You might think there wouldn't be much scope for revealing character in this limited setting, but there is plenty. People who take an aisle seat when the window seat is empty make anyone who comes later have to climb over them. People who put their backpacks on the next seat are claiming it. People who talk loudly on cell phones are claiming an even wider space. Any setting is fodder for character development.

Writing time!

- Write a scene imagining how the future dictator of the world would behave if left alone in someone's kitchen. Next, have her leave the kitchen to go somewhere on a train. Write her traveling etiquette. Picture her waking up in the forest with Yura. Write how she handles herself. Think of a few possibilities for each of these settings. Use any or all in a story.

- In a story you're working on now, or an old one, put your MC into an unfamiliar setting. Write how he conducts himself.
- In the fairy tale "Rumpelstiltskin," the imp is overheard by one of the queen's messengers as he sings a ditty about his name. Suppose the messenger watches him through his cottage window. Describe the interior of the cottage. Show him bustling about, in a benign way or a creepy way, preparing for the baby's arrival.

Have fun, and save what you write!

· SECTION THREE ·

Character Nitty-Gritty

· CHAPTER 10 ·

Like Me!

A confession: I've had trouble, more than once, making my MC sympathetic. And, since my misery loves the company of other writers, I was glad to find that some on the blog have had the same difficulty. For example, a writer called Gray wrote, "I have this fear of making my main characters unlikable."

Here's an example of how I've gone wrong. In *Fairies and the Quest for Never Land*, Gwendolyn, my MC, is a human girl who visits the fairies. When something bad happened to a fairy, I made Gwendolyn think about the consequences for herself and not about the poor fairy. I did this without realizing. After all, the effects on Gwendolyn were important! They were going to move the story along. But, alas, she came off as a selfish pig!

So how do we make our characters sympathetic?

A friend of mine, the delightful children's book writer Molly Blaisdell, once told me that if you make a character rescue someone else, he becomes sympathetic, at least temporarily. Sound advice. It doesn't have to be a big deal like pulling a baby out of the jaws of a man-eating shark. It can be tiny. For instance, after our MC Sandra sticks up for someone who's unpopular or transports an ant outside rather than killing it, the reader is going to be inclined in her favor.

That's not the only strategy. Think of real people you like and what you like about them. You can insert their qualities into your characters. Barry is completely dependable. Zelda thinks the best of everyone. Alice makes you laugh. And so on. There are many ways for people and characters to please us.

The tools that we use to develop characters are there to help us make them sympathetic. Rescuing is an example of action. Let's move on to some of the others: thoughts, feelings, speech, appearance.

If Sandra's thoughts are one long whine, the reader isn't going to enjoy spending time with her. Not that she has to be merry all the time. For example, as she's saving the ant, she can be annoyed at it. She can think, *Stupid bug. Step on the paper towel, you idiot. Don't make me beg.* The reader is likely to sympathize with her irritation.

While extending the paper towel, she can say, to amuse her younger brother who's watching, "Hop on, ant. This is your magic carpet. One giant step for antkind." Her brother giggles. She stops what she's doing to smile at him. Her words and actions have won the reader over. The smile even reflects her feelings. She's pleased to be entertaining her brother.

As for appearance, perfection is probably not as appealing as mild imperfection. Our MC can have a weak chin or oversized ears. When I created Aza in *Fairest*, I made her physically unattractive, but I didn't give her a terrible oozing rash or brown and crooked teeth, which might make the reader recoil rather than slip inside her.

There is no formula. If we work at it, we may be able to make the reader like a hideous-looking character. We like the Hulk, and we feel for Frankenstein's monster.

Oddly enough, the reader may have more trouble sympathizing with perfection. We don't like Superman for his looks; rather, we're won over by his hopeless longing for Lois Lane, the danger from Kryptonite, and Clark Kent's pathetic earnestness.

Some writers manage to pull off an unlikable but sympathetic main character. M. T. Anderson does it with Titus in his young adult novel *Feed*. Titus isn't likable—not to me, anyway. I pitied him, felt for his limited life, and wished futilely that his world would change—and couldn't put the book down. He's not even interesting; he's utterly shallow, which may be the point of the book. In this terrible world, no one can rise above circumstance to develop depth. But Titus pulls our heartstrings so hard they almost snap—and sympathy pours out.

Writing time!

- Four friends are hiking together. They run out of trail mix. One sprains an ankle. Rain starts to fall. Camp is still three miles off. Make them all deteriorate into annoying people. Create a crisis and bring them back to likable.
- Your MC Yvette is popular. She's with several of her friends at a dance. An odd, unpopular boy is there, too, and Yvette goes out of her way to be cruel to him. Write the scene and make Yvette sympathetic even while she's behaving badly. This may be hard; hints of her inner life—her thoughts and feelings—will help.

Have fun, and save what you write!

· CHAPTER 11 ·

To Change or Not to Change

In my early writing days I often heard the advice that a character has to evolve during a story, and the charmingly named Sage-in-Socks wrote in to the blog about exactly this: "Sometimes I find myself forcing a change in a character because I feel that, to be a round, dynamic character, he or she must change in some way by the end of the story. To what extent should a character change? Are subtle changes like a change of opinion also characteristic of dynamic characters? Or should a character by the end of the story be quite different from what he or she is like in the beginning? Are there any limits? I mean I wouldn' t want to 'force' a character to change or change her personality—I rather like their flaws."

Hooray for likable flaws! Our MC certainly shouldn't do a one-eighty. He still needs to be himself at the end. And the changes can be subtle. A change of opinion, maybe a new understanding of something—cultural differences, for example—may do the trick.

It probably isn't wise to force change on a character. Whatever growth comes about needs to arise from how the character acts in a situation and what she thinks or feels or says.

Sometimes the reader absolutely does not want a character to change. As a child, I gobbled up books in the Cherry Ames series. I did not want Cherry to switch even the color of her lipstick! I loved her exactly as she was.

This is true of some series today, too, where the characters can be counted on to carry their strengths and weaknesses from book to book. Mysteries often fall into this category; the detective is the constant. There are new crimes to solve, but the sleuth remains unaltered. I hope to write more mystery books about Elodie and the dragon Meenore. Elodie will probably grow older and change, but I plan to keep Meenore essentially the same.

Ella's character doesn't vary much in the course of *Ella Enchanted*. Because of her actions, her circumstances change, but she has much the same personality at the end as she did when her mother got sick. On the other hand, Addie, the heroine of my book *The Two Princesses of Bamarre*, is fundamentally altered as a result of her exploits, but I don't think I did a better job with one heroine or the other. Different stories have different effects on their characters. And the degree of change may vary too. In some stories a mere change of opinion will be exactly what's needed.

Like so much else in writing, it depends.

Some rounded, dynamic, actual people—you know them—never change. The aunt you count on to listen and not judge goes on listening and not judging for years. She is a rock. The cousin who criticizes everybody continues to criticize, no matter how his harping hurts his closest relationships. He is a rock, too, one with a painfully sharp edge.

Sometimes, failure to adapt will result in tragedy. In my novel *Ever*, Kezi's view of the religion she grew up in evolves. If she'd stuck to her original beliefs, she would have been sacrificed to a god who the reader comes to doubt. Even if Kezi herself wouldn't have, the reader would regard her death as a tragedy.

In a different story, tragedy might be averted by refusal to change. Suppose MC Marnie befriends a new boy at school. Let's call him Larry. At first Larry is well liked, but then rumors begin to circulate about him, serious stuff: he steals; he brought a knife to his former school; he lies about everything. When Marnie doesn't believe the rumors and continues the friendship, her other friends desert her, saying they're afraid of Larry and are becoming afraid of her. Even

Marnie's parents warn her against the boy, who is spiraling into depression. Marnie hangs firm, doesn't change; and her trust keeps Larry afloat against the accusations, which may be true or false. If they're true, Marnie may bring about change in Larry and help him become a better person.

Or Marnie is hurt, but she still concludes that she did what was right. Or *aaa!* Marnie is killed, and then her staunchness turns into a fatal flaw.

In some respects, Marnie will change whichever way the story goes. She'll learn more about her friends and about herself. She may have a greater moral sense by the end. In most stories, your MC will change at least a little. As the author, you can highlight the changes by having your MC reflect on them or having other characters point them out. Or you can simply show your MC behaving in a new way.

If Marnie, in addition to her faithfulness, interrupts people often or bites her nails or needs to sleep with a night-light, those aspects of her personality can remain untouched—or we can change them as evidence of her new maturity. But we probably don't want to change everything about her.

Writing time!

- Write the story of Marnie and Larry. Decide whether either of them changes. Show how it happens or fails to happen.

- Your MC wants to reform herself, to stop being bossy and become more caring. Write a scene in which she completely fails at this self-improvement.
- Superman gives up saving people. Write the turning point that pushes him in this direction.

Have fun, and save what you write!

· CHAPTER 12 ·

Villainy

Several questions have come in to the blog about villains, like this one from Jenna R.: "Does anyone have ideas on how to craft a believable villain?"

Actually, sometimes—in a superhero comic book, for example—a villain doesn't have to be believable. If Superman can change from meek and mild mannered to staunch and courageous just by changing his outfit in a phone booth, the villain doesn't have to have much depth or motivation either. This kind of hero is born good and the bad guy is born bad. As Kirk Douglas says chillingly in the old movie *The List of Adrian Messenger*, "Evil is."

Our villain may operate in the background of the story and never even show up in person. For example, in the Sherlock Holmes series by Arthur Conan Doyle, the reader never directly meets Holmes's archenemy, Professor Moriarty. In this bit of the story "The Final Problem,"

Holmes is speaking about Moriarty to Dr. Watson, his faithful assistant and the narrator of the series:

> *"He is the Napoleon of crime, Watson. He is the organizer of half that is evil and of nearly all that is undetected in this great city. He is a genius, a philosopher, an abstract thinker. He has a brain of the first order. He sits motionless, like a spider in the centre of its web, but that web has a thousand radiations, and he knows well every quiver of each of them. He does little himself. He only plans."*

Holmes goes on to describe a meeting he had with Moriarty, and the reader learns that the villain is tall and "his forehead domes out in a white curve," a vivid detail. But the man isn't shown in action or in his customary setting or in much conversation. He may boast to his accomplices or be silent for hours on end. His mansion may be filled with antiques, which he dusts to calm his nerves, or he may live in an attic and own no more than a bed and a dresser, and he may never be nervous. And so on. The ordinary clues that build a character are missing. Arthur Conan Doyle relies instead on the reader's imagination to make Moriarty threatening, and we jump in, building monumental evil.

When the reader does come face-to-face with a villain, however, he should be interesting. In my book *Dave at Night*, the main villain is the superintendent of the orphanage where Dave lives. He is a terrible man. His name is Mr. Bloom, but the orphans call him Mr. Doom. Here are snippets from his monologue before he beats Dave up:

> *Mrs. Bloom and I love the finer things in life, the theater, concerts. . . . Mrs. Bloom's little hobby is following the doings of high society. . . . So one might wonder at my choice of vocation. I admit it's a sacrifice, but someone has to do the dirty work. Someone has to take in children like you. . . . Otherwise you'd have nowhere to go. However, it's like putting a rattlesnake to your bosom.*

He's awful, but he has a personality, and the reader hates him even more for it.

Of course, in order for Mr. Bloom to be understood as evil, Dave has to be sympathetic. If he's a young thief who likes to rob old people, Mr. Bloom's sacrifice may seem real.

One way to craft a complex villain is through surprises. I'll show you what I mean.

Ordinarily the villain won't be our MC, so we probably won't have her thoughts and feelings to work with, but we do have all the other tools of character creation, like action, setting, appearance, and dialogue.

Let's call our villain Monique. She's already burned down a barn, a tree house, and the tree it was in, and she's plotting to set a series of fires in the nearby city of Makville. Some of the story takes place in her house, where the reader is surprised to discover that she collects teddy bears—and she doesn't hang them by the neck in her bedroom. She bakes cookies—not poisoned—for a homeless shelter and feeds oatmeal cookie dough to the family beagle.

In dialogue, she can be witty and interested in other characters, which may be creepy. When your hero says something that puts him at a disadvantage, Monique can astonish the reader by letting it slide—although she may use the information later.

We can reveal her diary, in which she writes only about her visits to the homeless shelter and nothing about her fascination with fire. Or maybe she alludes to it in a vague way, like "Mother scolded me today. I have no idea what she was going on about, but she was very angry."

Yikes!

Even description can make her more complicated—dark eye makeup with pink lipstick. Pudgy face, muscular body. Terrible posture. An unexplained bandage on her arm.

If Monique is sympathetic, there is a danger that the reader won't understand when she acts on her wickedness. He may think, "I identify with Monique, and I like her; I don't believe she'd behave so despicably." If we want to mislead the reader for a while, that's fine. But if not, the solution is to introduce Monique's evil side as soon as the reader meets her. We show her being awful, or we have a character the reader trusts talk about some vileness she's committed. Right from the start we've established that she isn't good.

The villain—or if not the villain, strictly speaking, the foe—doesn't even have to be a character; it can be a disease (as in *The Two Princesses of Bamarre*) or weather or a cosmological force. In Norse mythology, as I understand it, evil is destined to win eventually—not a particular embodiment of evil, like Loki, but evil itself. Political theories—communism, Nazism, to name two—can play the part of the villain.

The foe can even be a belief. I once worked with a man who believed himself unlucky. Whenever anything bad happened to him, he blamed it on his rotten luck. This belief robbed him of hope and stopped him from taking action to help himself. If he were my MC, he would be his own worst enemy. We see this kind of internal foe often in fiction. In superhero comics again, villains come and go, but loneliness is often the enemy that can never be defeated.

Although it's fine to create villains who are simply evil, diversifying is good. Try your hand at a sympathetic villain. Make her more than likable; make her lovable. Maybe she takes such delight in her dastardly deeds that we can't help but chortle along. Maybe he harms people, but his remorse makes us forgive him again and again.

When I was a young woman, I knew a real-life villain who had no one's best interest at heart but his own. He took people's money and persuaded them to devote their lives to him. He was wicked, but, oh my, he was fun. A conversation with him kept you on your toes and made you think. His sense of humor was complicated but not mean. At first I wouldn't get the joke; a few seconds would pass, and then I'd be laughing my head off. When he wanted to, he could make me feel as smart as he was, and when he wanted to, he could make me feel as dumb as a termite. He would make a great character. The reader would enjoy being in his company even while recognizing what a miserable person he was. So one strategy is to make our villain delightful on the page.

Most readers of *The Two Princesses of Bamarre* fall for the dragon Vollys even though she intends to kill the MC, Addie. Vollys's tragedy is that she always incinerates the people she loves. She traps them, comes to adore them, and spends every minute in their company until they start to drive her crazy. Then she kills them and misses them instantly and mourns them eternally.

One reason the reader loves Vollys is because she appreciates Addie, just as the reader does. That's a second strategy. If our villain hates the world with one exception, our MC, the reader will discount the world.

Vollys is also expert at showing her side of the story. Dragons and humans have battled for centuries. She reveals the dragon angle on the conflict so that the reader has to sympathize. Here are a few lines of the poem Vollys recites about her mother's death at the hands of a human hero, Drualt:

Swift-flying Hothi,
Slain by Drualt.
And Zira, flame
Of fury, young beauty,
Her he slew also.
Men call him
The Laugher, the Hero.
Drualt, stifling fire,
Snuffing life,
No hero to dragons.

So that's another strategy: to show events from our villain's perspective.

Even a whiny, annoying antagonist will be better tolerated by the reader if our MC loves him. Let's imagine that our MC, Thea, baby-sits a troubled seven-year-old, Ricky, who is in a terrible mood when the reader meets him. Thea may be mad at him, but she still loves him, and in her thoughts she tells the reader why. It could go something like this: "Thea sat back in the couch, stunned. When she'd told Ricky about feeling stupid, she'd never thought he'd use the information against her. From his triumphant face, she saw he'd been saving it up. Then he ducked his head as if he expected her to come at him. She saw the curls at the nape of his neck and his T-shirt label sticking out. Her fury melted."

Along the same lines—and this is one more strategy—an outside, omniscient narrator's affection for a character can make the reader like him. This is from *Peter Pan* again, a few pages after Captain Hook has wantonly killed one of his own pirates:

> *Hook heaved a heavy sigh; and I know not why it was, perhaps it was because of the soft beauty of the evening, but there came over him a desire to confide to his faithful bo'sun the story of his life.*

Later on, because of Peter's wiles, Hook believes himself to be a fish. Who can hate such a silly man?

Consider fictional characters you know who are mixed blessings but beloved anyway. Think about how the author has reconciled you to them. Go back to the books and examine the way it was done, the sentences and incidents that created the effect.

We don't need a villain or evil in every story. There's no evil when the enemy is a circumstance, like a storm. What there always has to be is struggle, something or someone our MC has to grapple with.

Writing time!

We're going to use clichés for these prompts. Clichés are expressions that we've all heard tons of times. They continue to be repeated because they get an idea across neatly and quickly. Some, like "blanket of snow," are just catchy ways to capture an image. But others, like "nothing ventured, nothing gained," have tremendous depth. They're great, except for the small detail of having been way overused. We're hauling a few in here for our villains.

- "Makes him (or her) tick." Visit your villain's childhood and write a flashback that shows how he became bad, or when he first acted on his evil.
- "Calm before the storm." Write a scene with rising tension that sets your villain off. Bring a victim into this scene.

- "Can of worms." The brain of a villain is likely to be an unpleasant place. Her thoughts may be different from the thoughts of ordinary people—more chaotic or more disciplined or more or less fully formed. What goes on in the mind of your villain? Write what she thinks before she falls asleep or when she wakes up or walks down the street.
- "24/7." Show how your scoundrel never has time off from his evil. Maybe as soon as he performs one heinous act, the urge rises to perform another. Maybe he ticks off his villainy the way we check off items on a to-do list.
- "World class." Show your evildoer getting the best of another stinker or a clever and powerful good opponent. Let your reader see what your hero is up against.

Now, put all or some of them together in a story.

Have fun, and save what you write!

·CHAPTER 13·

Creature Creation

Another kind of character needing development is the sort we're unlikely to meet in real life: beings such as fairies, elves, dragons. Elizabeth asked on the blog, "I'm working on a novella right now about dragons, Gail, and I was curious about your take on dealing with magical creatures."

(A novella, for anyone who isn't sure, sits in length and complexity between a short story and a novel.)

Since magical creatures don't exist—or I believe they don't—we can invent our own versions of them. Before I let my imagination run wild, I think about the role a particular creature is going to play in my story. I ask myself what this character will have to do and be.

Let's take dragons, since Elizabeth mentioned them.

In *The Two Princesses of Bamarre*, dragons are one of the species of monsters that plague the kingdom, so they can't be good. After I decided that, I worked on the form their evil might take. And that's the second question you can ask yourself. Evil, yes. But evil how? Use what we discussed in the last chapter: Simply evil, or evil in a complicated way? Sympathetic, yes or no? Likable, yes or no?

Suppose we want our dragons not to be villains, however. Suppose we want them to be allies of the tree-dwelling clan, the Opkos, against the cave-dwelling beetle people, the Ditnits. Lots of follow-up questions flow from this decision: How do the dragons help? Are these flying dragons? How smart are they? How do they communicate with the Opkos? Through speech or in some other way?

It's writing time! List three more questions you can ask about the dragons in this scenario. Answer them. Then write a scene involving the first contact between a main character of the Opkos clan and a dragon who is going to be important in your story.

As we progress in the writing, we may discover that we've imagined traits for the creatures that don't fit our plot as it develops, so we have to go back and revise, which is fine and necessary. This happened to me with tiffens, creatures I invented for *Fairies and the Quest for Never Land*. I got too elaborate, and some of the characteristics didn't work, so I dropped them.

At some point in the questions you asked yourself, you probably moved from plot demands to pure invention, another fun part of the process. For this, we can think about the usual portrayal of a creature and ask how we can diverge while keeping enough of its essence that it's still recognizable. There's a lot of leeway. For example, we could even get away with a dragon mouse—a scaly mouse with a long snout, and fire no bigger than a match flame. In *Ella Enchanted*, the dragon is a baby, tiny with a tiny flame.

Unless we're writing fan fiction, we should stay away from dragon representations we've encountered in contemporary books. Anne McCaffrey's series springs to my mind, as does Ursula K. Le Guin's Earthsea Cycle. If there are dragons in novels you've read, think about how you can make yours different. Let's take my Masteress Meenore from *A Tale of Two Castles* as an example. IT is a detective dragon. You can write a detective dragon too without stepping on my authorial toes, but don't also make IT stink of sulfur and refuse to reveal ITs gender and have gorgeous translucent wings.

I like a sense of wonder in fantasy. I achieve this in Meenore with ITs wings, ITs smoke that changes color according to ITs emotional state, and ITs facility at the game of knucklebones. So there's a new question: What is likely to astonish the reader in a good way?

Another consideration is the amount of power we're going to give our creatures. This often comes up with fairies, who can do anything in traditional fairy tales. Omnipotence (limitless power) can be a problem for us modern writers, because we don't want the fairies swooping in and saving our MC. We want her to save herself. So how much power do our fairies or dragons have? How does their power work? For example, for fairies does the power reside in the magic wand? Or in spells? Or somehow in the fairy herself? In my Disney Fairies books, the fairies' power is limited to their talents. The water talent fairies, for example, control only water. Also, the magic is enhanced by fairy dust; without the dust they're hardly magical at all.

Power for evil has to be limited, too. If our dragon is evil and can destroy everything and is unstoppable, there's no story. Our evil creature needs an Achilles's heel, a way she can be stopped.

We needn't limit ourselves to the standard roster of imaginary creatures, either. We can go to mythology for other kinds of critters, like the hydra, a serpent with nine heads. And we can create our own. Again, we think of our story and the kind of creature we may need. Do we want to make it up entirely or combine creatures? A coyote and an eagle? A boa constrictor and a hippo? If made up entirely, how big is it? What are its powers? Think of ten more questions you can ask about your new creation. Answer them.

Going against my usual method, let's not consider our story first. Instead, let's start with our creature and think of a tale to go with him. If we're taking this route, we'll begin with what his problems may be. Our next step is to figure out how he might approach the problems. Then, as in any story, our job is to make trouble for him and keep him from achieving his goals easily. So that's another prompt: Decide what your creature's problem is or what he wants. List several possibilities. Pick one and start your story. Keep going.

Have fun, and save what you write!

• CHAPTER 14 •

Creature Country

Okay, we have our critter. Now for its world, its setting, which can be ordinary and modern . . . or not.

It's writing time right off: A dragon or other magical creature of your choosing moves in next door to your main human character, who lives in a home very much like your house or apartment. This dragon arrives with a mission, a reason for coming. Your human character may want something, too—protection from a bully or friendship or a good science project or anything else you like. Write the scene of their meeting and bring the modern world into it. If you like, keep going. Write the whole story, the novel, or the seven-book series.

When I start writing a fantasy, I ask myself questions, write notes, make lists. What kind of universe is this? So far, most of my books have been set in fairy-tale land—several are sort of medieval, one is sort of ancient Mesopotamian, and one is modern except for a single witch. Next time, who knows?

I may ask myself, and you can ask yourself, Am I writing a drama, a love story, a tragedy, or a mystery? Or a funny story, which will call for a different, goofier universe than a serious tale.

What kind of characters inhabit this world? Fairies? Dragons? Philosopher eagles? A combo of different sorts of creatures? People? Animals? Or plants that have somehow become ambulatory and able to think and communicate? Rocks or paper clips? Anything can succeed if we make it succeed.

You can list some aspects of the real world that you love and aspects you definitely do not love. Long ago, I read a short story about an alien who adored Earth because we eat food. In his home galaxy there was no such activity. Our characters could enter a world without birds and any concept of flight, for example.

We can list the basics: size, time, light, colors, sound, smell. Write down how your world might express them. In Terry Pratchett's Discworld series, for example, light moves slowly. But Terry Pratchett doesn't change all the essentials, and we shouldn't either. Some—probably many—aspects should be what we're used to, or the reader will feel lost.

More writing time! Try creating a story in which all the characters are objects you find on your desk.

Realistic stories are generally (not always) set in places our readers are familiar with. Most people can imagine a school, a city street, a park. They won't visualize the exact school, street, or park that is in our mind's eye, but close enough. As we show the scenery and describe the important landmarks, our readers see the town or city or countryside.

There's less familiarity in fantasy, but there's some. If we're writing a medieval fantasy, most readers have seen enough movies and TV and read enough books to picture a castle, swordplay, tights and a doublet, or a princess gown. We don't have to say that a castle has towers and a moat, but if it lacks one or the other or both, the reader has to be told. Also, we need to show the setting, so even if the towers are ordinary, we may want to point them out the first time they come into view. They may add to the mood or have emotional meaning for our MC, by representing home or the enemy, for example.

Our readers are going to assume that the rules of our natural world apply to our story unless we tell them otherwise. We don't have to mention that the sun rises in the east and sets in the west and the sky is blue. But if the planet in our story has two suns, a green sky, and no moon, readers must be informed. However, when I write fantasy, I keep it as simple as I can and pity the poor reader who has a lot to follow. If I don't need a green sky, I don't put one in.

In my opinion, readers should be able to imagine our fantasy elements: see, hear, smell, and feel them. If something is invisible or inaudible, then the other senses should be recruited to fill in. I have no patience with silent, invisible force fields crashing into objects that also can't be perceived—unless the writer is being funny and I get the joke.

When I've set a story in a place that doesn't exist, I avoid identifying details that are closely tied to the world we all live in. I made an important dog character in *A Tale of Two Castles* be a Lepai mountain dog, a breed that readers won't find in any kennel club. If he'd been a poodle, the reader might be jolted momentarily out of the story, might think, *I have a poodle too! What kind of cut does this one have?*

The white people in my fantasies are never European; the blacks aren't African. There is no Europe and no Africa where they live.

On the other hand, when I had Kezi in *Ever* be a gifted weaver, I learned about weaving, because the process seems universal: fiber that has to be made into cloth. Maybe I could have made something up, but I didn't want to complicate my story.

At the beginning of this chapter we brought a dragon into a modern house, but often the process goes the other way. A human leaves home and enters an unfamiliar realm. How can we do this in an original way, without using a door, a mirror, a wardrobe, or a rabbit hole?

Well, the entry point could be connected to our MC's character. Suppose she's great at math, and one day she walks into math class and none of the problems add up. The teacher looks exactly like Mr. Mikan, except this Mr. Mikan has bushy eyebrows. She's in. That simple. I'd guess there are lots of ways to do this. I bet you can think up some right now. Look around, wherever you are. Listen. Sniff.

What might you change, what little thing—your cat reciting a nursery rhyme, the car you're in developing legs rather than wheels—that could plunge a character into strange and unknown circumstances? List three possibilities. Pick one and use it in a story.

More writing time!

- Invent a new imaginary creature, not a fairy or an elf or an ogre. Describe it. Put it in a story.
- I sometimes wonder how progress happened, especially early human progress. For instance, how did somebody realize that metal could be extracted from ore? How did farming start? Who invented shoelaces? I once read that in the Middle Ages buttons were purely decorative, sewn on clothing just to look pretty; they didn't fasten

anything. How did buttons migrate from decorative to useful? Imagine how something was invented without looking it up. Who was there? What was the dialogue? Was there an argument? Write the scene.

- Write dialogue among a statue, a river, and a jack-o'-lantern. Before you start, think about how each might express itself.
- Write a scene in which you introduce a fortune-teller and show the reader that his power is real.

Have fun, and save what you write!

·CHAPTER 15·

Love's Labor Found

I enjoy brewing up romance, but some on the blog struggle with it. When I want people to fall in love, I think of them as jigsaw pieces that need to fit together. This bit of him has to satisfy that place in her that's missing or has been starved, and vice versa. Maybe I see it this way because of my parents, who stayed in love for forty nine years until my father's death. My mom finished college (at the age of sixteen); my dad didn't complete high school, and he loved having a brilliant wife. He was smart, too, but very modest. My mother loved his innocence and sweetness. She could be a wee bit tart. He loved her complexity. They argued sometimes, but fundamentally they filled the crevices in each other that needed filling.

In my Princess Tale *Princess Sonora and the Long Sleep*, I echo my parents' relationship. Princess Sonora is the smartest person on Earth by a factor of ten. She's eager to share her knowledge, but no one wants to listen. Prince Christopher is curious about everything, and people tire of his endless questions. They're made for each other. In another Princess Tale, *The Fairy's Return*, Robin makes up jokes, for which he is scorned by his father and brothers. Princess Lark thinks his jokes are hysterical. Everyone treats her with kid gloves, which makes her feel stifled, but Robin doesn't. They, too, are primed for love. So one strategy is to think about what our characters may need and even crave.

Here's another: When you approach writing romance think of . . . your pet. A dog or cat needs care and calls on us for protection. That protectiveness is part of love, and a mutual part, too. The boy isn't always watching out for the girl; she's got his back, too. In *Ella Enchanted*, for example, Char shows up in time to keep Ella from being eaten by ogres, but she saves him and his knights by making the ogres docile.

Animals can't hide their feelings. We know when they're happy, frightened, stubborn, or jealous. We see them at their worst and love them anyway. They're naked literally (unless decked out in a vest or party hat!) and figuratively. Their openness makes us free. We tell our pets our secrets and let them see us cry and pound the pillow. This kind of intimacy and acceptance is part of love. In my novel *Fairest*, for example, Ijori is aware of Aza's self-loathing and loves her anyway, and she forgives him and loves him even after he lets himself be convinced that she might be part ogre.

Admiration can advance love. We usually think better of a person who thinks well of us, and so can your characters. In Jane Austen's *Northanger Abbey*, Catherine Morland admires Henry Tilney, and her admiration sparks his love for her.

And fun moves romance along. I just looked at the romantic moments in some of my books. The heroes and heroines are having a terrific time together. Mutual appreciation ricochets back and forth, and each character feels at his or her best, wittiest, most interesting, handsomest or prettiest, most awake, most alive when they're together.

Then there's the physical side of romance, the chemistry. The two can simply stand near each other and feel the air shimmer between them. Their eyes can meet. Eye contact is powerful and can be romantic if the gaze is soft. In a tender moment, a character can notice his breathing become shallow; another can feel warm in a chilly room. One or both can blush. I searched online for "signs of romantic attraction" and read that hair touching, licking one's lips, dropping the gaze and then looking back, and leaning toward the other person can be signs.

We can make up our own signs, too. Suppose Gloria has a tiny scar next to her right eye, which embarrasses her.

When she's attracted to a boy, she puts her hand on the spot to cover it. Then she thinks that may look silly, so she takes her hand away. We put her through this quick sequence a couple of times at a party to introduce it. (We don't want to overdo.) Then, two days later, she sits next to Jeff at a school play and does it. The reader understands instantly what's going on.

Or Jeff becomes clumsy in the presence of someone he likes. Stuart pulls his shoulders back and widens his stance. Sharyn rises on tiptoe.

Often it's an accumulation of incidents and character traits that produces like and love. Somebody says something that expresses exactly how you feel but have never been able to put into words, and you sense a deep connection with him or her. This may be trite, but a smile that lights up a face can flip my heart. Humor, as long as it's not at anyone's expense, draws me in, too.

Details count in writing love as in writing everything else. The reader needs to know exactly what the heroine said that flew straight into the hero's soul. And the reader has to be told enough about the hero to understand why he's so touched. For example, my late and much-missed friend Nedda often told stories on herself and laughed uproariously. I adored the stories and the loud belly laugh, but someone else might have been embarrassed by one or both.

If the romance in our story is just a subplot, the love can go well. But if the main event is romance, then we need trouble. The ending has to be earned with serious or comic misery. Jeff can be too shy to approach Gloria. Sharyn's parents can move the family to Belgium just when she and Stuart start opening up to each other. An old boyfriend or girlfriend returns. A misunderstanding occurs. Or anything else.

But the process is reversed in a tragic romance. In the beginning or the middle, we need joy, compatibility, delight in the loved one's company, along with hints that sadness lies ahead.

When we write romance, it's reassuring to know that the reader will do some of our work for us, because it is a truth universally acknowledged that the reader, upon encountering two unattached characters, will speculate about, and most likely wish for, romance between them.

I heart making people fall in love!

Writing time!

- Siderita is a dryad who's out of her tree for the first time in centuries. Zack is a modern city kid who's forest phobic. Write their romance. Try it from one POV and then switch.
- Invent a romance between Gretel, of "Hansel and Gretel" fame, and Rumpelstiltskin. She's smart and

fearless. He can spin straw and who-knows-what-else into gold.

- Hannah and Reed are at a party together. They've barely met, but their friends think they're perfect for each other. Make it all go horribly wrong. If you like, continue the story and end with a valentine.

Have fun, and save what you write!

· SECTION FOUR ·

Hatching the Plot

·CHAPTER 16·

Stirring the Plot

After character development, the second most frequent question on the blog has been about plot. Here's an example from Alexis: "I love writing, but I usually just write with very little in mind, typing whatever comes to me, and it ends up this elongated mess with no clear plot. When I deliberately set out to make a plot, I think of that chart I got in middle school, where I had to define the rising action and the climax and the falling action and so on. This just seems to take all the fun and creativity out of writing for me, but I know I just can't write blindly. Can you please help me?"

I'm a plot-driven writer. By plot-driven I mean that I develop characters based on where I want my story to go, rather than coming up with a character and finding my story by following her. Generally I start with an idea. For example, *The Fairy's Mistake* is based on the fairy tale "Toads and Diamonds," in which a fairy rewards a girl for a good deed by making jewels and flowers drop from her mouth whenever she speaks. The fairy punishes her sister for being unkind by making snakes and toads come out of her mouth. The sweet sister is further rewarded because a prince falls in love with her goodness and decides that the jewels can be her dowry. The unpleasant sister comes to a bad end because no one will go near her.

My big idea was that the prince would be unlikely to fall in love with this young woman in an instant, but he might immediately fall in love with the precious stones she's constantly producing. With that notion in mind, I made the prince a tad materialistic, the good sister unable to stick up for herself, the nasty sister quick to recognize opportunity when it exits her lips, and the fairy a failure at foreseeing the consequences of her magic. As the story barrels along, the good sister has to talk constantly and comes down with an awful sore throat. The bad sister gets anything she wants whenever she threatens to speak. And the fairy wrings her hands in distress.

So that's one plotting strategy. Think what might be your central idea. Then bring in characters who can carry your idea. This may take some doing. You may need to write a few pages of notes, but once you have two or three characters, figure out what they might do next and what the consequences could be.

Suppose this is where you are with your story: In real life you go to the doctor for a sore throat, and in the waiting room you see a worried-looking family. You don't know why they're worried, but you start making up a reason and writing it down, because, naturally, you have your notebook with you. You write that the night before, the son, who looks to be about fourteen, showed his mother a mark on the inside of his arm that had appeared just that afternoon. In real life, yesterday, before you got sick, you visited the ancient Egypt display at your local museum, so you decide that the mark is in the shape of a scarab—the beetle design you saw on Egyptian amulets. You imagine what happens when the nurse calls the family in. The doctor feels the mark, looks at it through a magnifying glass, is mystified, takes a small skin sample, and says she'll have the results in a week. The family leaves the clinic and on their way home the car has a flat tire, and for some inexplicable reason the wrench won't loosen the tire lug nuts, even after the car is towed to a mechanic.

At this point you feel the story getting away from you. You don't know what anything means or who anyone is. The scarab mark could be anything, and the car issue seems to have driven in from another tale.

Sit back and look at what you have, which is a lot of potential. What could be your big idea?

You start to write down possibilities. Here are a few that occur to me:

- The son has reached the age when the mind of a murdered pharaoh will wake up in him and seek revenge on the woman who took his life, who was prophesied to return in the same year he does. In the course of the story the original boy will assert himself from inside the brain of the pharaoh. The result will be something better than revenge.
- The son has a rare blood disease, and the mark is the first symptom. He has a week to live, but during that week he will become unnaturally strong. The ending will be bittersweet. The boy will die, but first he'll accomplish something important to him.
- The skin sample baffles the scientists in the lab to which it is sent. After everyone goes home that night, the sample begins to change. By morning it has taken on the appearance—and taste—of a cinnamon cake, which the scientists and lab techs are unable to resist, with strange and disturbing results. (They don't notice that the skin sample is missing.) Everyone eats except a single scientist, who is home with a cold. In the end, the scientist who was left out will realize what happened and will warn the world before being tempted to eat the cake too.

Writing time!

Your turn. Write down four more possibilities, including

at least one that involves the car and the flat tire. With each possibility, tentatively make up an ending. Then, for the ones that interest you, including mine, consider how you might develop the characters to move the story forward in the direction of that ending. For example, do we need the scientist who didn't eat the cake to be a suspicious soul? Will he catch on quickly that something is odd when he returns to the lab? Or should he be so focused on his own experiments that he hardly notices anyone else? Maybe initially he escapes the cake through luck and obliviousness.

Write the story.

Your decision about the ending may change as you go. That's fine. It's there mostly to give you a direction.

Notice that when you pick one of your ideas, you may have to cut a lot of what you've already written. That's common; it happens to me often. In your writing life you may toss out enough words to fill a big bookcase. I probably have. It doesn't matter. They're just words, and a lot of them are *the* and *of* and *and*!

However, I save my snips, the sentences or paragraphs or pages, in a folder I call *Extra* in case I need them again. I have Extras for every book I've written, and occasionally they've come in handy.

More coming up on plot. In the meantime, have fun, and save what you write!

·CHAPTER 17·

The Plot Thickens

Sometimes I get lost.

To find my way in my story, I write notes about where I am and where I might go. And I show my efforts to my writing buddy, the excellent writer and illustrator of books for children and teens Karen Romano Young. Sometimes she has ideas about how my plot can move forward.

So these are two more plot strategies in addition to finding your central idea: notes and showing your story to a trusted friend or adult, someone you can count on to give constructive criticism and not to make you feel bad, not to say that what you've done is stupid, or worse, that you're stupid.

I have more suggestions, but first let's talk about plot itself, which arises out of character and situation, usually a difficult situation. Take the first possibility in the last chapter, the one with the ancient pharaoh. The situation is the return of this dead dude who takes over a boy's being and wants revenge. We know little about the former pharaoh, just that he was murdered and that, thousands of years later, he's still ticked off.

What else can we come up with for him? What was he like in his day? How old was he, for one thing? I would probably make him fourteen, too, the same age as the boy he invaded, so they have that in common. But age isn't much to go on. What else? Let's say the young pharaoh was assassinated after he'd sat on the throne for only a few months. Was he kind or despotic? Did the kingdom rejoice or mourn when he died? Did he have a sense of humor? Happy humor, or did he make fun of people? Was he stubborn or did he give up easily?

While you're thinking about him, keep part of your mind on the modern boy. The two need to correspond in more than age. I don't mean they need to be similar, but some traits in the pharaoh should link with some in the boy, either by being opposite or by being similar.

Once you have an idea of the boy and the pharaoh, you'll probably want to move on to the pharaoh's murderer and the modern-day girl she's entered. Ask yourself questions about them.

You'll need more characters, of course. You can think about them now or when you're ready to bring them into your story.

Try this method on any of your tales that have wandered around and gotten lost. After you've decided on your big idea, tweak your characters so they can move it along. Then return to your story, which should have begun to take shape.

Another approach to plot, often mentioned in books about writing, is to ask yourself what a character wants and erect barriers to her achieving her goal. An example of this is Jerry Spinelli's Newbery Honor novel, *Wringer*, about Palmer LaRue, a boy who doesn't want to participate in his town's annual pigeon shoot. One of the obstacles is Palmer himself, who hopes, despite his reluctance, to be accepted by the boys who do participate.

Then again, instead of asking what your MC wants most, you can ask what she fears most and make it happen. Now she's in a terrible situation. What does she do about it?

Many plots *can* be described according to that middle-school chart, as rising action followed by crisis, then falling action, and finally resolution. This sequence works for lots of writers. Let's look at "The Three Little Pigs" as an example. In the rising action each pig builds his house and the wolf does his powerful blowing. In the crisis the wolf comes down the chimney of the brick house. I'm guessing that the falling action is when the wolf gets boiled, and I suppose the resolution is when the pigs congratulate each other and the first two swear to use only brick when they rebuild.

To try this method, think about what the problem will be, how you can make it worse-worse-worse, how you can bring it to a head, and then how you can solve it, which doesn't necessarily mean solving it happily. I did this in *The Two Princesses of Bamarre*, in which Meryl, the sick sister, gets sicker and sicker, while Addie fails at her every attempt to find the cure.

Sometimes in a tragedy matters get better and better during the rising action, and then in the climax everything falls apart. An example of this is the Greek myth about Orpheus and Eurydice. They're newlyweds when Eurydice is bitten by a viper and dies. After that, matters begin to improve. Grief-stricken, Orpheus, a gifted musician and singer, travels down to Hades, the world of the dead, to perform for the gods and persuade them to let his wife live again. He's told she can follow him back to life. Hooray! But he mustn't turn to look at her until they've climbed completely out. He waits until he's reemerged, but when he turns, she's still in shadow, and—*boom!*—he loses her forever.

Not all stories follow the rising action/crisis sequence. For example, Louisa May Alcott's *Little Women* doesn't. Lots of crises happen, but I'm not sure which is the major one or what resolves the book. There's Jo's relationship with

Laurie, Beth's health, the family's poverty, the challenges that each sister presents to herself. That's four, and I may have missed some. And yet, when we come to The End, we're satisfied.

A book can be organized to take place during a particular time and place, like summer camp or a wilderness adventure. Joan Abelove's young adult novel *Go and Come Back*, which I quoted from in chapter 8, covers a year in the life of a teenage girl in the jungles of Peru. It begins when two American anthropologists come to live in her village and ends when they leave. During that time, she saves a baby, one of the anthropologists gets very sick, a turtle is washed with surprising results, and much more.

In a story such as *Go and Come Back*, this happens, that happens; maybe there's a crisis, maybe not. But events unfold. Friendships may be made and even lost. Skills are gained. The MC comes away changed, and the reader is satisfied.

However, even if you're writing this kind of tale, your plot will need emotional ups and downs. Your MC has to be at least a little miserable at some point.

To create that misery, think about what interests you in your story. What's the trigger? Suppose you've put two friends in a park and you don't know what to do with them. Hunt for a spot where you can make trouble. You don't have to crack the earth open, revealing a thousand monsters snapping their jaws (although you can if you want to). The misery may be the tiniest thing. You can just have one character—let's call her Willa—say to the other, "I hate when you do that." Nobody likes to be criticized, and you can intensify it. Willa's friend Abigail answers, "And I hate when you watch my every move just waiting for something to criticize. At least I don't do that." Willa says in angry triumph, "You just did!" Abigail can march off, and Willa can text something that she will quickly regret to someone they both know. Your story is off and running.

It's writing time!

Here's another line of dialogue that can create big trouble: Make one character ask another what she's thinking, which can be a very bad question, depending on what the other character has on his mind and how honest he is. Create some kind of disaster—interpersonal or global or intergalactic—as a consequence.

Have fun, and save what you write!

·CHAPTER 18·

Have at It

Every summer I teach a creative writing workshop for kids, and I always start by asking what they'd especially like to learn. One recent summer the answer was that they wanted to learn how to write conflict.

Cool! We all need to write conflict.

But I'd never taught the subject, so I did an online search for "conflict in fiction" and discovered a list of four kinds of conflict:

- Character versus other character (interpersonal).
- Character versus same character (internal).
- Character versus nature.
- Character versus society.

I rolled the last two together into character versus situation (external).

Character versus character needn't only be human against human. There's also human against alien or fairy or vampire, or human-altered-through-mutation against ordinary human or fairy against fairy. But the clash must be up close and personal, not between battling armies. The characters should be sentient (thinking). Conflict between a human and a shark—unless it's a brainy, talking shark—would fall into the character-against-situation category.

The conflict between characters may be big or small, over the future of mankind or whether or not to get a dog. It can be played out in words or in deeds. For example, in deeds, Eric might maneuver so that Victor is unable to audition for the school play, or so that he can't find the formula that will destroy the world.

Opportunities abound for internal conflict. A character can argue with himself about a fear, a fault, an ethical decision, a career, a menu choice at a restaurant. We've all experienced some of these. Sometimes I can get frustrated with myself. Why can't I decide?

There are zillions of examples of character against situation, among them a forest fire, slavery, homelessness, and a dictatorship.

We don't have to limit our story to one kind of conflict. Our MC Ira can argue with his friend Jenna and then with himself over the same subject, how to help mistreated dogs.

The story can be primarily about animal cruelty (character against situation) or friendship (interpersonal) or Ira's fear of taking action (internal).

Writing time!

Here's a prompt that involves character versus situation. A hurricane hits town. Carlie is at a friend's house when the storm hits. The power goes out. Her dog, who is terrified of thunder, is home alone. Carlie decides to go home to comfort her pet. Write what happens. Make the reader worry.

This one uses internal conflict. You may know the story "The Lady, or the Tiger." If you don't, it's basically this: A princess, who has a jealous nature, falls in love with a man below her station. The king finds out and arranges a punishment for her beloved. He's thrown into an arena with two doors. Behind one is a beautiful maiden and behind the other a tiger. If he picks the door with the maiden, he lives, but he has to marry her. If he chooses the door with the tiger, he gets eaten. In the arena he looks to the princess, who knows what's behind each door, for a signal. She has to decide whether to endure his marriage to someone else or to condemn him to death. The story has no ending; the reader is asked to decide what the princess will do. When the man enters the arena, the two characters, separately, experience severe internal conflict. The princess is arguing with herself about which door to point to, and the man is arguing with himself about whether to believe her signal when it comes. Write the thoughts of one or both. If you like, continue and invent an ending that reveals the outcome. (To do this, you may have to bring in more characters, write the events that landed the man in the arena, and deepen the characters of your two MCs.)

This one coming up is one of my favorite prompts of all time. It features a car trip, a great place for interpersonal strife. You can drag in the other kinds of conflict, too. We all have different driving styles and different styles of being a passenger. And think of the radio! Or CD player or iPod, or DVD player in the backseat. What kind of music to listen to? Who prefers news or a recorded book? Open window? Closed window? How high to crank the heat or the air conditioner? Who sits in front? Does anybody get carsick?

And what about the car itself? Are soda cans rattling around on the floor? Does the car smell like the family dog? Or does it still have a new-car smell after two years? Is it in good repair? Is it a junker? Does it have a spare tire? Jumper cables?

Here's the prompt: Perry is invited to vacation with his best friend, Letty Pewer, and her parents. They are traveling from Minnesota to Florida for a winter week in the sun. Below are some possibilities to fool around with. Pick as many as you like or make up your own or do a combo of mine and yours. Bring in details of your own terrible car trips. Whatever you choose, write the story.

- Letty's father is peculiar. You decide how.
- Letty's mom is a dangerous driver. You decide how.
- Letty's younger brother and older sister are coming, too. They don't get along with Letty and dislike Perry.
- The car is older than Perry. The radio doesn't work. There is no iPod, no CD player.
- The Pewers are economizing and haven't bought a GPS. Paper maps are good enough for them. They plan to camp out and save on motel costs as soon as they reach warm enough weather.
- The car is bewitched—not in a good way.
- This is the snowiest winter in the history of Minnesota and surrounding states.
- The scenic route will take the family and Perry through an old mining town. Unbeknownst to the authorities, one of the abandoned mines is now occupied by squatters, who may be dangerous.

Have fun, and save what you write!

· CHAPTER 19 ·

Nail-Biting

Okay, we've got conflict, essential for an exciting story, but Grace commented, "I still struggle to heighten the tension."

Here are ten ways to do that in no particular order; some are driven by situation, some by character:

1. Time pressure. Not every story has it; not every story needs it. But if time pressure comes into the plot naturally, hooray! The clock ticks. The reader's heart pounds—if he remembers. Our job is to remind him. The deadline, whatever it is, has to loom, which we can accomplish by various means: with count-down chapter headings; in worried thoughts; in scenes that show how unprepared our MC Fiona is; in dialogue, when a tutor, for example, reminds her how few days are left until the exam that will determine her fate.
2. A milestone. Fiona is traveling toward some important

destination—a long-lost parent, a new home, the answer to a mystery. In this case, the chapter headings can be miles remaining or train stops to go. The reason that makes the destination critical can be told in flashbacks along the way.

3. Thoughts. If Fiona worries, our reader is likely to worry too. We don't want her to worry obsessively—unless that's what she always does—but we do want to drop in a few thoughts about possible disaster every so often. As an added benefit, worries are a great way to end a chapter when we don't have an actual cliffhanger handy.
4. Nonstop action. A chase story would be an example of this. Fiona is pursued by a villain who's after the golden charm on her silver charm bracelet, which was given to her at birth by an eccentric aunt. As soon as she thinks she's escaped, the villain pops up again.
5. Separation from the problem. Suppose Fiona, whose enemy is Luke, has to go on a class wilderness week. What is he doing while she's away? What's going to greet her on her return? If we aren't writing in first person, we can even show what Fiona is going to walk into. Of course, the wilderness week has to be interesting too.

In *The Two Princesses of Bamarre* the MC, Addie, sets out to find the cure for her sister's fatal disease.

While the two are apart and when Addie is deprived of her magic spyglass, she keeps worrying that her sister's condition has worsened. I wanted the reader to worry too. What if Meryl has already died?

6. A flaw in your MC. In *The Two Princesses of Bamarre* again, Addie is a coward. The reader fears that she won't find the courage to help her sister.
7. A flaw in a secondary character. Suppose Fiona's boyfriend is treacherous or unpredictable—kind one minute, mean the next. His character flaw is a source of tension. Any sort of flaw can work: forgetfulness, clinginess, selfishness, stinginess, and so on. We simply have to set it up so that Fiona needs something that the flawed character can't be counted on to supply.
8. Isolation. Fiona can wander away from the other campers in her wilderness group and get lost. Wildcats live in these hills. Their habitat is shrinking, and they're hungry. *Aaa!*
9. Expectation. Mom expects Fiona to be a brilliant student in every subject. Or, going the opposite way, Mom always expects her to fall short. Her best friend expects her to sacrifice her needs for his again and again. Or Fiona has hard-to-live-up-to expectations of herself.
10. Injustice. Fiona has been falsely accused. She's misunderstood. In my book *Dave at Night*, Dave's precious carving of Noah's ark has been stolen. Much of the

book's tension comes from the search for it and worry about the repercussions that may follow its recovery.

Reread a few books that you couldn't put down long enough to brush your teeth. Study the author's suspense techniques and see how you might apply them to your story.

Tension is particularly needed when we close a chapter. A good chapter ending makes the reader want to—have to—keep reading. More than anywhere else in a book, the chapter ending has to compel or tempt the reader forward, because otherwise that page turn is such an invitation to turn off the flashlight under the covers or to answer all those text messages that have been piling up.

One fundamental principle underlies chapter endings: something should be amiss. If one problem has been solved, another should rise from the horizon or come forward from the background.

How to achieve those irresistible last lines or last paragraphs? I've gone through my *Fairies and the Quest for Never Land* for some of the ways:

- A cliffhanger. A chapter in *Fairies* ends with my MC, Gwendolyn, falling out of the sky toward a circle of sharks with their mouths open.
- Worry. The second chapter ends with Gwendolyn worrying that Peter Pan will forget to come for her. The worries of

a sympathetic secondary character will do also. In *Fairies*, I ended nine out of thirty-two chapters with a worry.

- The villain is plotting or doing something awful, unbeknownst to your MC. We can show this only from a third-person POV.
- The beginning of a major event. Peter does come for Gwendolyn. I end the chapter in which he arrives at the moment before the two meet.
- A single powerful word. Chapter 8 ends, "Then a new miracle began." *Miracle* is the magic word. Of course what follows has to live up to the promise, has to be a miracle, even if a minor one.
- An emotional moment. Suppose your MC has just unwittingly insulted a friend. The chapter can end when he realizes what he's done, before the friend has reacted, because anticipation is a crucial factor in chapter endings.
- A threat. After the unwitting insult, the friends argue without reconciling. The chapter ends with the hurt friend saying, "I'll get you for this."
- A surprise. The readers' suspicions are lulled. Things have been going pretty well. Someone shrieks. End of chapter.
- The absolute worst happens. End the chapter. But the absolute worst can't happen many times in a single book. You can get away with a few absolute worsts, but probably not many, unless you're writing over-the-top comedy.

I'm sure there are more terrific ways to end a chapter, and you'll find ones that particularly suit your book. Be on the lookout for them as you write.

And, to close with the obvious, a book doesn't have to be organized into chapters. *P.S. Longer Letter Later* by Ann M. Martin and Paula Danziger is an epistolary novel (a novel in letters and other documents), in which the breaks come at the end of each letter. *Monster* by Walter Dean Myers is written in the form of a screenplay. Anne Frank's *Diary of a Young Girl* is made up of real diary entries. Some books are a hodgepodge of letters, notes, newspaper articles, journal pages, as well as narrative.

Writing time!

Tension can enter just about every situation. Here I am, typing at my computer. Suppose the words that appear on my screen aren't the words I'm typing. I would freak out, and a reader probably would too. So the prompt is: As you do whatever you're doing today, think about how each action (putting on your socks, eating lunch, passing a store window), or each place (your bedroom, classroom, local park, a city street) could be suspenseful. Write down the ideas that come to you. Use one or more of them in a story.

Have fun, and save what you write!

·CHAPTER 20·

Plotting Along

A plot type that I find easy to work with is the quest. In *Ella Enchanted* Ella is on a quest to end her curse. In *The Two Princesses of Bamarre* Addie quests to find the cure to the Gray Death and save her sister. In *Ever* Kezi's quest is simply to survive. A quest can be for a greater good than merely saving our MC or a single person she loves. In *The Lord of the Rings*, for example, the quest is to destroy the ring of power lest all Middle-earth be taken over by evil Sauron.

The goal is paramount in a quest story. To try one, think of your MC's objective. Make attaining it hard-hard-hard and make her fail-fail-fail until, for a happy ending, she finally succeeds, or, for tragedy, she's defeated for good.

Notice that I wrote both *hard* and *fail* three times in the last paragraph. Three is a useful number in plotting, so useful that it has its own rule, called the rule of three. When your hero strives to overcome an obstacle, try giving him two attempts (using different methods each time) before he succeeds. Three is often a satisfying number. Cinderella goes to the ball three times. The evil stepmother visits Snow White in the forest three times. The queen guesses Rumpelstiltskin's name three times.

Not always three, however, or the reader will be able to predict what's coming. Sometimes your hero should succeed on his first shot and sometimes on the fifth, and sometimes not at all, at least for the time being. Variety adds richness and interest.

The circle is a satisfying plot shape, too. This kind of story ends where it began, as in *The Lord of the Rings*, *The Wizard of Oz*, *Peter Pan*, and my book *Fairy Dust and the Quest for the Egg*.

Setting takes on special importance in these tales. *Peter Pan* would lose all its magic if there were no Neverland, and the suspense would disappear if there weren't the tension between the island and the ordinary, grown-up mainland.

Although a circular story returns to its original setting, the MC is usually changed by what happens in the middle. Frodo, for example, is quite a different hobbit when he returns from Mordor. Dorothy returns from Oz with a new understanding of herself and an appreciation for her aunt and uncle's farm. But your MC may not change, and the story can still be wonderful. Wendy changes by the end of *Peter Pan*, but Peter doesn't, and we don't want him to. We love him as he is, conceited and lighter than air.

Let's leave shape behind and try this plot tactic for a floundering story, which can be done with a pen or using computer software. Here's the old-fashioned way: Try writing a short summary of each scene on an index card, then spread the cards out and move them around, altering their original sequence. You can even bring in scenes from other unfinished stories. Edgar in your old story can turn into Garth with a few personality adjustments. When you think about the characters, do you see new threads that connect them? Does one scene suggest itself as a fresh beginning? Another as the end? If your story flows except for a few scenes that stubbornly don't fit in anywhere, you can cut them and move them to your Extras folder.

If you find that the cards move you further along but then you bog down, you can lay them out again starting with the point where you got stuck—you don't have to go all the way back to the beginning.

And here's a plot exercise that comes from *What If? Writing Exercises for Fiction Writers* by Anne Bernays and Pamela Painter. You can use it on a new story or an old one. If this is a new story, whenever you're not sure where to take the story next, ask yourself *What if?* In your notes write down five options for directions the story might take, within the confines of your big idea or use this method to help you discover the big idea, which we discussed in chapter 16. Be wild. Be carefree. Don't even look at what you have till you're done.

It might go like this: My MC is at a party and feeling all alone. *What if* she sees a framed photo of her long-lost brother on the mantelpiece? *What if* she starts writing on a wall of the living room where the party is happening? *What if* she decides the party needs livening up and starts singing? And so on.

Now look over your list. Suppose two options appeal to you. Write a paragraph about each, what it would mean for your story, how it would take place. Pick the one you like best and return to your story. If you reach the next story decision point and you're not sure, ask *What if?* again and repeat.

Writing time!

- This familiar lullaby is totally crazy (and creepy), in my opinion:

  Rock-a-bye, baby, on the treetop,
  When the wind blows, the cradle will rock,
  When the bough breaks, the cradle will fall,
  And down will come baby, cradle and all.

Who put Baby up there? Does somebody want to kill her? Turn this one into a story or a novel.

- Pick a secondary character from one of your old stories and make him the MC in a new one. Ask what he fears most. Bring his worst fear down on him. Write about how he responds. Does he overcome? Or, if you're writing a tragedy, does he succumb?
- Take the humor road with a disaster deluge. Write a story that involves the end of civilization, lost love, drowning rats, a curse on green-eyed men, and the spontaneous combustion of umbrellas! Handicap your MC with double vision, an inability to pronounce the letter *t*, and a fear of metal. Or make up your own disasters. This is the silly side of storytelling.
- Your MC sets out in this circular story, taking his dog (or other animal or creature) for a walk. What sparks the adventure? What gets in the way of his return? How does he get home again (because a circular tale always winds up where it began)? Write the story.

As you get ready to write, consider where your MC lives. In a city? On a farm? In a suburban subdivision? Dog walking is going to be different in each. If this is a fantasy, your MC could be walking a young unicorn from rock to rock in a swamp inhabited by I-don't-know-whats.

Also think about time period. Nowadays, people in many places are required by law to pick up after their dogs. That wasn't always true. Dog walking itself is probably relatively new. I suspect people in the Middle Ages didn't do it. If your story takes place during pre–dog walking history, invent a reason for this unusual activity.

Have fun, and save what you write!

· SECTION FIVE ·

Aspects of Story

·CHAPTER 21·

Midstory Crisis

The biggest chunk of plot, the place where we're most likely to get lost, is the middle. A writer called Unsocialized Homeschooler said this about the problem: "I wonder about middles. I always have some sort of ending in mind when I start writing, and beginnings are usually easy for me, but it's the middle that's the hardest. Getting from point A to point C is always rough for me, and I can't just skip point B. Some people have told me to take a while and outline everything, but I'm not a fan of outlines, and they don't seem to work for me.

"Does anyone have any tips for getting through sagging middles?"

There are two secrets to middles. One lies in our characters—main characters and secondaries. We'll start there.

Let's look at middles in fairy tales, stories with the

simplest of structures. Here are the beginnings and the ends of a few.

Beginning: Evil queen discovers that Snow White has surpassed her in beauty and is overcome with jealous rage.

End: Evil queen dances to death in red-hot shoes at the wedding of Snow White and the prince.

Beginning: Cinderella's father marries a horrible woman with two equally horrible daughters, and Cinderella is made the servant of this terrible trio.

End: Cinderella marries the prince and forgives her stepfamily.

Beginning: Sleeping Beauty's parents fail to invite an unforgiving fairy to the christening of their daughter.

End: Sleeping Beauty wakes up to a kiss by her prince.

In each of these we could drive a herd of cattle, a circus, and a marching band between the beginning and the end, meaning that almost anything could happen. Neither the middle nor the end is made necessary by the beginning. Let's take the most complex of the three, "Snow White." To get to the end and to fill up the middle, the inventor of the tale in the mists of history hauled in a magic mirror, a kind-hearted hunter, seven dwarfs, and a prince—and gave the queen a few witchy powers.

Seeds for the middle and the end lurk within the character of the queen. She's furious, but she doesn't slip into

Snow White's bedroom at midnight and bludgeon her to death. Maybe she's afraid of being caught, or maybe even she shies away from that degree of violence. She wants the awful deed done, but she doesn't want to do it herself—at first. Her unwillingness moves the story along.

The next seed is that she's a bad judge of character. She doesn't notice the hunter's kindness or the admiring glances he bestows on Snow White.

Snow White herself isn't much help. She's little more than a pretty chess piece who moves from place to place merely because she's pushed. When she's abandoned in the forest, she walks—I'll give her that. And she stumbles into the dwarfs' cottage. You know the rest. The dwarfs warn Snow White of her danger, but she's too stupid or foolish to listen. The queen overcomes her squeamishness about violence, decides to do the job herself, and finally seems to succeed. Then the dwarfs' love for Snow White causes them, weirdly, to put her in a glass coffin. Finally we have a prince who, weirdly again, falls for a seemingly dead maiden.

The point is, the story moves forward through the middle because of the characters.

Let's look at my version, *Fairest*, which progresses because of the characters. For starters, MC Aza dislikes her appearance and tries to alter it. Then there are the secondary characters. Behind the scenes are the parents who abandon her and set her story in motion. And there are the innkeepers who take her in and mold her into a young woman who, although insecure, knows she's loved and has solid values. We also have the duchess, who can't go to a wedding without a servant; a prince who has an eye for the exotic (Aza); a king who loves his wife; an insecure and jealous queen; an evil creature in the magic mirror; and, way behind the scenes, a crazy fairy. They all, directly or indirectly, rub against Aza and, because of their complexity, create the scenes that make the plot seem to rattle along but actually slow the story's progression with interesting moments and surprises—a satisfying middle.

Here's the second secret, which has to do with our ending. What we need to do when we enter our middle is to forget about the end with ninety percent of our brains. Only ten percent of our mind can have its eye on the finish line.

Let's try it. In our imagined beginning, our MC Beryl's village has been destroyed by war. Her parents were killed, and her brother and sister were taken by the army. Let's say Beryl is fifteen, old enough to have been taken, too, but she was missed because she was visiting someone on the village outskirts. She's left behind with the elderly, the sick, and the very young. Rebels prey on skeletal villages like hers. The survivors have to get to safety. We know that in the end Beryl and at least a few of the others will make it to some haven or other, although we don't know exactly what that will be.

We've written the beginning, in which Beryl returns to the center of the village and discovers how bad matters are. We look around with her and consider what other characters we might need. Well, we'll probably want one or two who can help her and one or two who will make her task much tougher. For the ones who can help her, there could be a child who has a hidden strength and an elder who has past experience with the methods of the rebels. For the ones who get in the way, one could be too sick to move. Another could disagree with all of Beryl's ideas and could divide the villagers. We might want to figure out a way to include a rebel or two in our cast. Maybe Beryl goes spying or a lone rebel is caught by their sentry.

We've got quite a bit of middle going already. The very ill character gets a scene or two, likewise the one who pits characters against one another. Beryl may be slow to realize that the child with the special strength (whatever it is) has it. The one with experience may be reluctant for some reason to share. Beryl's spy mission could run a dozen pages. The rebel who's caught becomes part of the action.

There can be natural crises, too—a hurricane, a blizzard, earth tremors. Food can run short. More food can be discovered. In each of these developments, the characters will respond characteristically. There won't merely be a hurricane, there will also be characters behaving foolishly or bravely or brilliantly—or all three—in the face of it.

It isn't enough to grasp what the characters' roles will be in our plot; we have to develop them, too. For example, the character who has had dealings before with the rebels can be truthful but long-winded, and she may demand to know the reason behind every question. Beryl will need qualities that help her and others that get in her way. Maybe in the past she's always given up too easily. She's distracted by grief for her family, but she's a good listener, and she has hunches that usually pan out.

As we're fooling around with all this middle stuff, we have an eye out for the route that will lead the villagers to safety, but we also have in mind that some element of the safety should be surprising. Safety, yes, but not exactly in the form the reader expects.

Writing time!

- Tell Beryl's story, changing any elements or characters you like. Go for at least five scenes in the middle.
- Expand "Sleeping Beauty" and keep the fairies who come to the christening on the scene. Have them and other castle characters get involved in creating a middle. Remember, in the fairy tale there's an ongoing effort to

keep Sleeping Beauty from pricking herself. Decide in a general way how you'd like the tale to end. You aren't locked into the long sleep and the big hedge and the prince.

- Retell any fairy tale you like, but make it modern and have it take place in an acting troupe or a circus or a dance school or any other situation that will bring a bunch of characters together. Again, keep your plans for the ending indistinct. See if you surprise yourself.

Have fun, and save what you write!

· CHAPTER 22 ·

Looking Back

The Queen of Hearts—let's call her Queenie—in Lewis Carroll's *Alice in Wonderland* specializes in shouting, "Off with his head!" Or her head. The reader is never told why.

If we want to spin our own tale from the original and the reason for the decapitations becomes important, then we need a way to reveal it.

The backstory and the flashback are two possibilities, both of which have come up on the blog. For example, MNM wrote, "I've been working on a story that is written in first person and I'm having issues with putting in the background or writing flashbacks."

The advantage of both backstory and flashback is that they add complexity and give our story a sense of depth, a layered feeling. *Fascinating!* the reader thinks.

The disadvantage is that we have to pull the reader out of the ongoing tale into the past. Then, once we've gotten her there, we labor to excite her interest, but we don't want her to fall so much in love with the past that she's unhappy about leaving. And when we do return to the present, reentry can be bumpy since she has to get immersed all over again.

Still, we can do it. We just have to set things up. Let's start with a flashback and see how we can accomplish it smoothly.

Suppose Queenie likes to behead both people, like Alice, and live playing cards because of a childhood tragedy. Her father, Daddy Card, the late King of Hearts, was assassinated, stabbed in the neck, eek! The assassin was never found, but the chief constable and Queenie are convinced he or she is still at court. We want the reader to understand Queenie and sympathize with her, so we decide to show what happened.

Here's how we might work it. (What follows is my creation. Lewis Carroll, who may be spinning in his grave, had nothing to do with it.) Queenie is in her bedchamber when a Nine of Clubs, a servant, brings in her mail, among which is a letter in a pale purple envelope. See how we go into the flashback:

> *She stared at the envelope on her dressing table. Her heart pounded. Daddy Card liked to write lengthy letters to family and friends on pale purple stationery—not this exact tint, but close. Hands trembling, she*

picked up the tiny silver dagger she used as a letter opener, and thought, Twelve years ago next month.

That day she had been in this room, too, opening replies to invitations to her eleventh birthday party. She had issued eighty-nine invitations, and eighty-nine children had accepted. As she'd been mounding the responses in a triumphant pile, feet had thudded in the corridor outside. She hardly heeded—the servants were always rushing about. Then came a soft knock, her lady-in-waiting's shy tap, but an instant later the woman entered without permission.

Notice that I started with *had been* and *had issued*, but switched to simple past in the sentence *She hardly heeded—the servants were always rushing about.* That sentence marks the complete shift to the earlier time.

The flashback continues. We see the shaken maid delivering the terrible news. Whatever ensues comes next: weeping, rushing out of the room, going to Mommy Card. Finally we bring Queenie back to her bedchamber and start the return transition:

She sat dully at her dressing table and stared without comprehension at the party replies. Oh, she finally remembered, the girl she used to be was going to have a celebration. For the first time, on that sad, long-ago day, she had collected her hair in a bun at the back of her neck, in the style of a grown woman. Then she had scattered the party responses onto the floor.

The mauve envelope in her hand now was unrelated to a party. There was no party. She hated parties. Who would be stupid enough to choose this color?

And we're back. I repeated the tense switch on the return with the sentence *For the first time, on that sad, long-ago day, she had collected her hair in a bun at the back of her neck. Then she had scattered the party responses onto the floor.* Two techniques make the transition smooth: the tense shift and an action that bridges the gap in time, in this case opening the mail.

But suppose we don't want to interrupt the story and we still want to provide the history. What are our other choices?

We can start our story at an earlier time, with the death of Daddy Card, continue to a scene or two from Queenie's later childhood, maybe including the first time she issues her execution cry. Then we jump forward to the present, in which most of the story takes place.

Or suppose Queenie always touches her throat before calling for an execution. If her husband, Kingie, the King of Hearts, who thoroughly understands his wife, manages to put his arm around her quickly enough, she relaxes and doesn't give the order. A newcomer to court can observe this and ask a friend to explain. In a short bit of dialogue the backstory of the father's assassination can be revealed.

Or, if we're writing from Queenie's POV, the reason for the beheadings can be revealed in thoughts, as in *Ten years coming up in a month. I was nicer before Daddy Card's assassination*.

Then we go back to the action. Five pages later, she might think something else, like *Dr. Two of Spades says I lost my father at a girl's most sensitive moment, no matter how he died. What a fool he is.*

She makes a weighing gesture with her hands and thinks, *Disease . . . assassination. Disease . . . assassination. Not the same.*

More action. Later on she can finish the backstory by thinking, *I probably killed the assassin long ago, but as long as I'm not sure, as long as he or she could still be playing croquet, I'll keep the executions coming*.

If we're writing from another character's POV, that character can be present for one of Queenie's execution orders and think about the past in a sentence or two.

Or the reader can do without the backstory. Everyone knows Queenie orders people's heads off. It's one of the facts of her reign. People avoid playing croquet with her and are terrified when they have to. If she's an important character, we can show her touching her throat, loving Kingie, seeming relieved when her husband pardons people. She'll come off as a complex character. Excellent.

Suppose we need the backstory of the whole card kingdom, not merely of Queenie's personal tragedy. Let's suppose Alice has a mission in Wonderland. In order to have a chance at success, she has to understand the place. One way would be to have her find a tome about it in her parents' library, and we can put a page from the book right in the story. We can have her stop in the middle to gasp or to get a glass of water, because when we break up the backstory with action in the present, we avoid suspending the forward tale for very long. For suspense, we can have her leave the room for the water and find the book gone when she comes back. She knows part of the story and she has to find out the rest, which moves the backstory into the front story. She can ask a historian, and we can include their conversation in our narrative.

Generally, we don't want to start a backstory or a flashback in the middle of an exciting moment. Notice that we began Queenie's flashback in her bedchamber, where not much is going on.

Writing time!

- Write the backstory that explains the history of the card monarchy. Were they people who were transformed into cards? Or has it always been this way? Who was the first ruler?
- Try your hand at interrupted action. The White Rabbit descends into his hole and dashes along the tunnel below. Move into a flashback that explains his hurry. In Lewis Carroll's story, he and Alice separate and the story follows her. Stick with him and invent what happens after the flashback.
- Make up a backstory for a character in a book you love.
- Ina is a writer. Whenever she meets people, she makes up their backstories and sometimes she forgets they aren't true. She's having dinner at her new best friend's house and meeting his family for the first time and inventing secret pasts for each of them. Write the scene and make the imagined backstories get her into trouble.

Have fun, and save what you write!

·CHAPTER 23·

Peering Ahead

In the last chapter we looked back over our authorial shoulders. Now let's put on our spyglasses and peer ahead. *Foreshadowing* is what peeking ahead is called, and it's another way to crank up story tension.

Many great books, especially old books—classics, even—warn the reader of future catastrophe. We might see something like *Dear Reader, If I had known in 1842 what I now know in 1862, I never would have entered Tabitha's Tea Emporium on that fateful July day.*

Here's an example from *Peter Pan*. It takes place in the Lost Boys' underground home in Neverland:

> *And then at last they all got into bed for Wendy's story, the story they loved best, the story Peter hated. Usually when she began to tell this story he left the room or put his hands over his ears; and possibly if he*

had done either of those things this time they might all still be on the island.

Contemporary stories don't usually use foreshadowing as directly as this, unless the writer is being funny. A humorous example might expand on what I wrote before, as in, *Dear Reader, If I had known in 1842 what I now know in 1862, I never would have entered Tabitha's Tea Emporium on that fateful July day and would have been spared many sleepless nights and a right earlobe the size of a grapefruit.* If we sprinkle silly foreshadowing like this in at regular intervals, the reader will be looking for it and laughing in advance.

Sometimes we can be tempted to use outright foreshadowing to prop up a dull part of our story. Things are slow right now, so we let the reader know that the action is going to pick up. Fred is eating a PB&J sandwich. A yawner, yes? So we tell the reader that the sandwich will lead to dire consequences. Sometimes this works, but it can be awkward. When a narrator addresses the reader, she takes him out of the immediate moment in the story. If the book is told by a first-person MC, the reader is reminded that the character isn't participating in events as they unfold but looking back on them.

Instead of a pronouncement about the future, we can skip the PB&J entirely or make the sandwich eating itself interesting.

There are more subtle ways we can suggest trouble to come. In both *Ella Enchanted* and *Fairest*, gnomes are prescient; that is, they can see into the future, although their future sight is dim. Their prophecies make the reader worry without interrupting the action. Dreams, too, can augur ill. In *Jane Eyre* by Charlotte Brontë, for example, dreaming of a child portends misfortune. The first instance of this comes when Jane's governess dreams of a child and soon learns her sister has died. Later, when Jane has such a dream, we tense and wait for the worst.

Dialogue foreshadowing can set off nail-biting. For example, Ron Banks-Butler is talking to Hallie Butler, his older cousin, who's two grades ahead of him in high school. Hallie asks him who his history teacher is going to be when school starts next week. Here's what follows:

> *Ron shrugged. "Mr. Twillet. Is he good?"*
>
> *"Twillet doesn't know what good means, and he has it in for kids with two last names."*
>
> *"What does he do to them?"*
>
> *"You don't want to know. It will just give you nightmares."*

Uh-oh.

Or we can use setting. Clara is boarding an airplane in

winter. The pilot announces that they have to wait while the ground crew deices the wings. Finally the plane begins to taxi, but Clara sees out her window a slick patch on the wing. She's sure it's ice. When she points the patch out to the flight attendant, he tells her everything is fine.

Uh-oh.

Or a character's past can ring a warning bell. Clara survives her flight, although at one point the plane drops precipitously and the oxygen masks come down. She's traveling to spend a week with her Aunt Flora in Florida, and the reader knows Aunt Flora suffered a psychotic episode as a young woman. Aunt Flora meets Clara's flight; she's where she should be, at baggage claim, and she's smiling her usual warm smile. Clara's eyes travel down to her aunt's feet. Her right foot is in a sandal, her left in a sneaker.

Uh-oh.

There's a famous writing principle called Chekhov's gun. The Russian author and playwright Anton Chekhov wrote, "If you say in the first chapter that there is a rifle hanging on the wall, in the second or third chapter it absolutely must go off. If it's not going to be fired, it shouldn't be hanging there."

A gun, or a rifle, is a significant object, unlike, say, a painting displayed on the same wall, which may be there just to provide insight into the character of the homeowner.

But when the reader sees that gun, she's put on notice. The gun triggers (pun intended!) the *uh-oh*. In the case of Aunt Flora's footwear, the reader will be disappointed if nothing comes of this strange fashion statement.

Writing time!

- Fred is eating that PB&J sandwich. Without announcing in the old-fashioned way that disaster lurks, make the reader uneasy. Maybe the jam tastes faintly bitter or Fred smells smoke or he hears a crash coming from the basement. Jot down a few possibilities or go with one of mine and write the story.
- Continue the saga of Clara in Florida. Is Aunt Flora descending into insanity again, or is there another explanation for the mismatched shoes? What will Aunt Flora do next?
- Ron, who's nervous about starting school and encountering his history teacher, walks his dog, Shadow, the night before. Get Ron out of having to go to school, but not in a good way. In fact, make school look much better than the trouble he and Shadow land in. Before the misery strikes, give the reader hints that something bad is on the way. Write the story.

Have fun, and save what you write!

·CHAPTER 24·

Mysterious

Have I mentioned that I love to fool my readers?

A great way to fool them is with a mystery. I bring this up because Amanda posted this comment: "I'm thinking about writing a mystery novel, but I've never written a mystery before. Do you have any tips on how to write one?"

At the heart of every mystery is a *who* question. It's the reason a mystery story is also called a *whodunit*.

The crime can be anything from murder to betrayed friendship to a stolen cupcake. More questions follow *who*? Why was the crime committed? What was the motive? How was it done?

In my mystery *A Tale of Two Castles*, Count Jonty Um, the victim, is hated by all the citizens of the town of Two Castles, and the reader doesn't know whom to trust. But we could go the other way. The victim could be beloved by everyone. Who would hit such a saint over the head? Or steal from him? Or spread lies about him?

All the citizens are too many suspects for our reader to keep track of. Three or four or maybe five are plenty. We can narrow the field simply by using our authorial spotlight. The characters we shine our beam on become fishy to the reader; the others we ignore, and so does the reader.

Is this fair? Maybe not, but we're in charge and what we decide rules.

As we write, we pile on puzzles and clues and red herrings (false clues that are meant to confuse the reader). In *A Tale of Two Castles*, several characters wear rings and bracelets made of twine. Narrator Elodie wonders if they belong to a secret society. A character who presents herself as poor is seen buying an expensive bracelet. A honey-tongued man speaks harshly. A gate is left open. An ox is mauled.

Even in stories that aren't primarily mysteries, there are likely to be puzzles. Somebody dislikes Mack, our MC, and he wonders why. His sister keeps coming home late from school and won't say what she's doing. His father stops playing the piano, which has always been his great joy. When asked, he says he'll get back to it, but months pass without music.

We can plan out our mystery ahead of time or we can solve it along with our sleuth. I've done the latter. When I wrote *A Tale of Two Castles*, I didn't know who the villain was until I'd written two-thirds of the book, which worried me, as you can imagine. But then this character did something revealing, and I knew, although the reader didn't yet. The advantage of discovering as we go is that the bad guy's identity may come as more of a surprise to the reader if it was also a surprise to us. The disadvantage is that we can lose our way for a while, which, sadly, has happened to me more than once.

Even if we've outlined and have settled the mystery for ourselves, our detective—let's stick with Mack—doesn't know who the perpetrator was. We want him to find the evildoer, so we have to help him, but we don't want to make it easy, either. How can we do that? Here are some ways, and I bet you can come up with more:

- The nature of the crime itself can help lead to the criminal. If our dastardly deed involves great physical strength or, going the other way, small stature, some suspects will be eliminated. (Or a clever villain may use these limits sneakily to direct the investigation away from her.)
- We can switch POVs. Carmella, the victim, knows a small piece of the puzzle; her cousin Nora knows something else. The villain knows most of all, and we can

tantalize the reader with tidbits from him. One charm of this POV-switching is that the reader learns more than Mack knows, which creates tension. *Oh, no,* the reader thinks, *watch out, Mack! Look under the bed!* But Mack has no reason to look, and so the reader suffers. Yay!

- We can give Mack particular traits that help him figure things out (a brilliant brain, extra-sharp hearing, understanding the speech of animals, or whatever else we come up with). And we can also handicap him in some ways (a habit of insulting people, physical weakness, sleepiness, or anything else) to increase reader anxiety. As an example, suppose Carmella is poisoned at a party. She's in the hospital, recovery in doubt, and the poisoner may strike again. Thirty people attended the party, including Mack. His special advantage is that his mother is a pharmacist who's shared facts with him about poisons, so he has knowledge to guide him.
- The setting can provide clues. Suppose the crime isn't poisoning. It's the theft of a famous painting from a museum. What's the museum's security system? Where was the painting hanging? Where does the guard usually stand?
- The nature of the victim can also lead to the perpetrator. In the poisoning scenario, is Carmella well liked? Despised? Rich? Poor? Kind? Mean? Does she have

enemies? On the day of the party, did she say anything odd? Did she seem different from her usual self?

- There are the obvious questions asked by detectives: Who benefits from the poisoning? The villain may gain if Carmella dies or may benefit simply from breaking the party up. Who was present? Who may have seen something suspicious?
- We, in our wisdom, can plant physical evidence. At the party, for instance, Mack can find a bowl with a few drops remaining of a greenish, smelly liquid.

Mystery readers pay attention to possible villains. Some will hope to identify the villain before Mack does. Our job is to prevent them from doing that. We want to produce the villain the way a magician pulls something surprising out of a hat—not a rabbit but a dozen butterflies.

Let's imagine that Mack investigates and we help him pick out four likely suspects. We'll name them after herbs and spices to make them easier to keep track of: Clove, Basil, Parsley, and Oregano.

If Clove is unpleasant, the reader may think, *It will be too obvious if Clove did it. She can't be the thief.*

If Basil is nice, the reader may think, *He's too sweet to poison anyone; he can't be the one—except maybe the author will think I won't suspect him, and he really did do it.*

If it turns out that Basil is the villain, the reader will think the outcome was predictable and be disappointed. If Clove did it, the ending may feel too easy. Maybe Parsley is the right choice. She wasn't at the party, but she hates Carmella, and Mack figures out how she could have gotten the poison to Carmella via Oregano, who had no idea Parsley was using him. The reader is amazed. Cool!

Mysteries with a detective combine two stories: the story of the crime and the story of the sleuth. In such tales, the MC is generally our detective, in this case Mack, and most readers will care more about him even than about the mystery. If Mack hardly knows Carmella and he's trying to find the poisoner's identity just out of curiosity, well, many readers may yawn and close the book.

But we don't want to lose them! How to pull them in?

Suppose Carmella is Mack's sister or his best friend or his girlfriend. He loves her and he's frantic over her condition and desperate to discover who means her harm. She's essential to his well-being. The reader is *not* yawning.

Or suppose Mack has a lot riding on solving this case. Maybe his friends have stopped believing in him. Nobody will ever ask him to solve anything again if he doesn't succeed now. He's even losing confidence in himself. The reader is eagerly turning pages.

For extra tension, although this won't work in every mystery, the villain can turn his attention to Mack when he feels Mack closing in. Now our hero himself is in danger. Oh, no!

In some mysteries our MC is the victim. Carmella recovers from her poisoning but knows someone is out to get her. There is no Mack. It's all up to her. The advantage here is that we don't have to juggle two tales, and our heroine is constantly at risk. The disadvantage is that we don't have the pleasure of creating a master sleuth and showing him work, unraveling clues, setting traps, confounding everyone—and making mistakes along the way.

So both are fine. Your choice. Or write one sort and then the other.

Writing time!

- You may know the kids' game "Who Stole the Cookie from the Cookie Jar?" One child after another is accused. It goes like this:

  "Who stole the cookie from the cookie jar?"

  "Maddie" (or the name of any child present) *"stole the cookie from the cookie jar."*

  "Who me? Couldn't be. Wasn't me."

  "Then who?"

  Another child is accused and the game continues until everyone is named. Turn the cookie theft into a story and solve the mystery. The trouble, of course, is that the most important evidence has been eaten.

- Mack's dalmatian has been kidnapped while Mack was visiting a friend and his parents were at work. Their house has an alarm system, which was not set off. A ransom note was left on the kitchen table. Write the investigation.
- Hope's younger sister, Eva, has gone missing, and the police are beginning to fear for her life. Eva was last seen on her way to a tutoring session with algebra teacher Jim Kilcannon. Hope visits Mr. Kilcannon's home to find out if he has any ideas about what may have befallen her sister. Write a scene in which you make Hope and the reader be alternately creeped out and reassured by Mr. Kilcannon. Use the setting as well as Mr. Kilcannon himself. If you like, keep going for a full-fledged murder or kidnapping mystery.
- Pick one or more of these scenarios from earlier in the chapter to write about and solve: Somebody dislikes Mack and he wonders why. His sister keeps coming home late from school and won't say what she's doing. His father stops playing the piano, which has always been his great joy. When asked, he says he'll get back to it, but months pass without music.

Have fun, and save what you write!

· CHAPTER 25 ·

Stranger Than Fiction

There's an adage for writers: "Write what you know." Let's look at it in light of these questions from a writer called Le, who wrote, "I have an idea for a fiction novel, but the inspiration for the story is from my own life. Some of the characters I want to put in the story will be similar, but not exactly like people I know. Have you ever done this? Have you used people you know as inspiration, and if so, have they noticed they are similar to your characters? Were they happy about this, or offended?"

Naturally, what we know best are our experiences and the people around us. There's nothing wrong with using them. Real people are great as a boost for concocting complicated, interesting characters almost instantly, and autobiographical fiction is no less an act of creation than making everything up is.

Years ago, I contributed a story to a book about grandmothers, called *In My Grandmother's House*. Most of the pieces are reminiscences. The contributors may be some of your favorite authors, such as Beverly Cleary, Diane Stanley, and Jean Craighead George, and you may want to know about their grandmas, who were almost all delightful and loving, and skilled cookie bakers.

I imagined an evening at the apartment of my grandmother and my two aunts. (I had only one grandmother, since my father was orphaned when he was very young.) Although my story is fictional, the evening could have actually taken place. Grandma's gambling loss really did happen—she always lost. I disliked her and my aunts, who were all mean to my mother.

They were dead by then, likewise my parents, but my mother's brother was still alive, and I didn't want to hurt him, so I told him about the project. He was horrified that I thought he might interfere with my creativity and told me to go ahead.

I did not ask for permission from his children. If they objected, they could write their own stories. Writing the piece was surprisingly moving, especially bringing my parents back to life. Details flooded in, with help from my sister, and I re-created our family in the early 1960s.

No one has ever complained.

Intention counts. I didn't write the story to be unpleasant or to hurt feelings. If you're respecting the real people, if you're even honoring them, they're likely to be pleased. They may feel important and be impressed that you paid attention. Joan Abelove, who had a brain injury a few years after writing her books, likes my poems about her even though they often mention the downside of memory loss.

I have gotten into trouble on other occasions. I named an MC in one of my books after a family member. I meant it as a compliment, but she didn't feel complimented and didn't tell me. I found out years later from someone else. I named the fairy Rani in the Disney Fairies series after my sister, who gave me permission, but then she wasn't happy about some of the shenanigans her namesake got into.

There is also the issue of invasion of privacy. Along these lines, Mya wrote on the blog, "I've had a few incidents happen in my life that are definitely out of the ordinary and involve love. I'm just dying to pen it all down, but I wonder how I should do so, without making it obviously similar to what really happened, so that I don't feel like I'm offending the other people's privacy. Any help?"

I wrote that opinions differ.

Say, for instance, that in real life Isaac kissed Ondine tentatively, a quick peck. Then, say, Ondine set down her big yellow purse for a longer, more satisfying meeting of the lips. Just as her arms went around Isaac's neck, a three-legged dog ran off with the purse, and a chase through Riverfront Park ensued.

Later that night, Ondine told her friend Ana the whole story, which ended with the recovery of the purse but no more kisses.

If Ana asks and gets permission from Isaac and Ondine to write the incident down, even to post it on her blog, she's home free, even if Isaac's dad isn't happy when he reads the post. But if she posts the story, names included, without asking, I say it's an invasion of privacy, whether or not Ondine said the anecdote was confidential.

However, some people disagree with me. They believe that the price of friendship or even family connection with a writer is the chance of appearing in print. Writers write, so this reasoning goes, and everything is fodder.

Now let's say Ana loves Ondine's anecdote and she's a writer but also a loyal friend. She lets a year go by, then writes a short story that revolves around this incident, but she changes the names of the characters. The story is one of her best, and it's published in a magazine neither Isaac nor Ondine nor any of their friends or relatives are likely to read.

Is this okay?

I think so, as long as the names were changed. It's certainly fine if Ana calls Isaac Anthony and Ondine Sonya and she has Sonya kiss Anthony first, and Anthony sets down his leather briefcase, which is taken by a three-legged coyote on 169th Street in New York City. Ana has definitely changed more than enough to protect the privacy of the real players.

In Ana's case, she may have improved the story by altering it, which often happens. We cast about for ways to change the events without losing their essence, and ideas pop up that add interest. Sometimes the essence actually becomes more concentrated. Real life meanders. Fiction is tighter.

We can also combine true stories. Think about dramatic or funny moments in your life and in the lives of people you know. Ask your parents and other relatives for incidents. Ask friends, teachers, librarians. List what you get and stare at the list. Maybe you've got these three that appeal to you more than any of the others: The first time Daryl met Frank, he had a hamster poking out of his shirt pocket. When she was four, Hester fell off the swings at her playground and landed on her head, which, she says, explains a lot. Joanne backed her car into a police car the day after she got her driver's license.

What can you do with them? Can you combine them into an entirely new story?

In a new scenario, suppose you rename Vince, your real friend, Samuel and turn him into a character, keeping everything about him the same, except for his appearance and his habit of yelling, "Shark sushi!" whenever he's surprised. Once you throw him into new situations, you're not invading his privacy. As soon as he acts in circumstances that you've invented, he becomes your creation.

If you're afraid of hurting feelings, you can discuss what you're planning with the people involved. You won't know their reactions until they react. One person may be flattered, someone else insulted, and then you can decide what to do. But you don't have to tell if you're changing the characteristics that will clearly identify them (like the "Shark sushi" expression) and moving events around. You can even deny. Without too much wickedness you can say, "You think you're like that? Huh! How fascinating!"

It isn't hard to disguise people. If you make Vince short when he's tall, give him a talent for the accordion, and have him be deathly allergic to peanuts, you are home free. Besides, it's likely that if you write your characters precisely as you experience their real-life counterparts, they won't recognize themselves. The girl you know is beautiful may see herself as ugly, or she may not be aware of how smart she is. The person who truly is a miserable human being will very probably not see himself in the villain unless you give the villain his first and last name.

If you are combining characteristics of real people—Melanie's generosity with Bill's habit of never covering his mouth when he yawns with Pam's inability to apologize—you are on entirely safe ground.

One more consideration, however: You also want to protect your own privacy. If you're basing a story on your own experiences, you can fictionalize yourself, too, especially if you're planning to post it online and your tale contains anything you wouldn't be proud for important people in your life to see. Change your name, your appearance, your gender, *your* habit of shouting "Shark sushi!"

Having said all this, life is an author's source. Don't hold back from dipping into the well.

Writing time!

- Write a memory as if it were a story. Make up the missing bits. Take yourself back to the moment with sensory details: what you see, hear, smell, touch. Include the mood and your thoughts and feelings. If you like, extend the memory beyond what you recall into a fictionalized future. Invent an ending.
- Think of a time when you were victimized, maybe teased or ganged up on. Replace yourself with someone you know. Write how that person would have handled the situation. Make it into a story.
- Ondine's friend Ana posts the kiss escapade on her blog. Ondine is merely furious, but Isaac, also a writer, starts typing his revenge. Write what he writes and what ensues.
- Write, solely for yourself, a true story you have no business sharing with anyone. If you feel like being mean,

be mean. If you have feelings that might not meet with general approval, include them. The process may bring relief, if you're describing an incident that caused you pain. Hide what you've written where it won't be found, but save it. A day may come when no harm will be done by sharing. And you may want to look at it now and then.

Have fun, and save what you write!

·CHAPTER 26·

Theme Park

I'm taking a new crack at a question from a writer named Pororo. My blog answer was somewhat different, but I've done more thinking since then. Here's the question:

"Do you have any suggestions for themes? For example, I read a story, and the theme was that once you have a dream, chase after it as hard as you can and that there's no such thing as a foolish dream.

"That kind of theme. I would like my story to be inspirational to someone like that story was inspirational to me."

I suspect we have a moral and not a theme on our hands here, so let's look at the difference, and let's take "Little Red Riding Hood" as an example. Its theme, I'd say, is a child's first adventure alone in the world. The moral that was delivered to me when I was six or seven was: Don't talk to strangers.

So theme is the idea—the gist, the thrust, the core—that runs through a story.

Moral is the lesson the story delivers, or that the author intends it to deliver.

I've begun to think about my next novel, and for it I'm researching the history of Jews in Spain in the Middle Ages, as I mentioned in chapter 2. The reason is that my father's ancestors were thrown out of that country along with all Spanish Jewry in 1492. I plan to write about it through fantasy, but the theme will be prejudice that takes the form of expelling a population from a kingdom.

So if you're looking for themes, mull over what's important to you. Casting my mind back to when I was about age fourteen, here are five themes that I could have based stories on:

- Being influenced—how my mother's worries got in my way.
- Friendship—my best friend, Beverly, and the fun we were having.
- Unpleasant people—how horrible my grandmother and my aunts were.
- Romance—my wish for a boy to like me romantically.
- Failure—how ashamed I felt about being terrible at volleyball.

I did write a story about one of my despised aunts. I never would have written about the fourth wish—too embarrassing!

Time to write!

Make a list of at least five possible themes for a story. Include your obsessions—the topics you can't stop thinking about, no matter how hard you try. Put down subjects you talk or text about again and again with friends. Add in things that seem to happen to you more often than to other people. Don't leave out themes that embarrass you.

A neat aspect of writing about themes that are important to you is that they're likely to be important to other people as well. If I write a story about stinking at volleyball, some readers may have the same problem, and even more will connect because of a different skill they can't master.

The next step is to develop the theme into a story. A real instance of my mother's fears influencing me happened when I learned to swim. My mother worried that I was going to drown, and her fear infected me so much that I floundered in the pool at camp the next day. A lifeguard had to rescue me.

But that's just a memory. To turn it into a story, we have to invent an MC. Let's call him Taylor, and let's stick with swimming. He's just made the swim team. Tomorrow is his first day of practice. Ordinarily he's not a worrier, and he's not worrying about swimming either—until the morning, when he talks to his older sister, who reads the daily horoscopes in the newspaper and believes them completely. It could go like this:

Taylor went into the kitchen thinking that scrambled eggs—the protein—would be great for his swimming performance.

Isabel, newspaper at her elbow, looked up from her bowl of cereal. "You had a great day yesterday, right?"

Taylor nodded. The swim team.

"Yesterday your horoscope predicted Pisces people would achieve a goal. Today it says that danger lurks." She deepened her voice, sounding like an oracle, and read, "Take no unnecessary risks." In her ordinary voice she added, "Aren't I a good sister to look out for you?"

"I'm not worried." Taylor took the egg carton out of the refrigerator. Wrong choice? he wondered. Carbs might be better, or maybe he should just have celery and shed a few pounds. He shook his head, trying to rid himself of the feeling of uncertainty.

This is just a snippet of what might be a story. We need something that went before about the swim team, and then we have to write how it plays out at the swimming pool. But, depending on what else we do, we've established our theme: that worries can be contagious.

As I said, I would have been embarrassed to write a romantic story, but probably because I wouldn't have known how to disguise it to eliminate my self-consciousness. I wish I could go back and tell myself. Luckily, I can tell you.

The character who wants romance doesn't have to be human and could be a mouse, a fox, a dragon, an elf, even an inanimate object. For example, *The Dot and the Line* by Norton Juster is the tale of a dot and the line who is madly in love with her.

To further lessen our discomfort about exposing our feelings, we can separate the tale from our ordinary environment. We can set it somewhere distant in place, time, or imagination. If we do all this, the theme may still hold a germ of embarrassment but little more, and that germ is likely to make our story extra exciting.

But suppose we want to write about a particular theme and we don't have any real-life associations to help us? How can we move from theme to tale?

Let's return to the theme of being influenced. The first step is to write notes to find our story problem. We ask ourselves what trouble being influenced might cause, and we list possibilities. Here are a few:

- An ill-intentioned person might persuade our MC to do something wrong.
- Our MC might get an idea from a book and try it out in real life with unfortunate consequences.
- Our MC might overhear a conversation, misinterpret it, and be moved to action.

Writing time! Jot down two more ways influence could cause trouble.

Next, we think over our choices and select one. Then we proceed to the character development stage we just discussed. Who is our MC? If, for instance, we picked the first option, who is that cunning character who set our MC on the path to no good?

After that, we have to work out the circumstances and imagine the scenes, just as we needed to do with Taylor.

More writing time! Pick one of your themes and decide on an MC. Consider the setting and the other characters and how they might be different from people in your own life. Start writing.

The moral—the lesson—of a tale about influence might turn out to be: "Hold fast to your core idea of yourself."

We could start our writing process just as we did with themes, by listing morals. But I don't recommend it. Morals can straitjacket a writer. Here's how:

Suppose I decide to write a story with the lesson "Study hard to get ahead." At the beginning, MC Otis doesn't prepare for an exam and he does poorly. He fails to get into a writing program that he knows he would have loved. The awakening comes. Otis recognizes that he should have studied instead of throwing a ball for hours for his new puppy to chase. He writes a letter of apology to the writing program, asking if he can retake the entrance test. His appeal is granted. He devotes all his waking hours to study and does well enough to be accepted. The story ends when he takes a seat in his new classroom, vowing to work just as hard now that he's here as he did to get in.

Please don't get me wrong—I definitely believe students should study hard. That's not the problem. I guess this is an okay story, but it's predictable and boring. We can guess early on that Otis is going to reform and do better. As I wrote my summary, I weeded out any possible complexity, because I wanted my moral to come through powerfully. So I didn't talk about the puppy who suffered from Otis's neglect and peed in the house as a result. And I certainly didn't include people who study hard and still don't get into programs they're longing for. I made Otis succeed because that outcome drove my moral home.

How much more interesting my story might have been if I'd just started with a theme about studying and made Otis be torn between playing with his adorable new puppy and preparing for an important exam. Then I could have followed my characters: the puppy; Otis; his parents, who have differing opinions about the writing program; and his older sister, who tends to criticize him.

As a reader I'm not fond of stories in which the moral dominates. I don't read fiction to be lectured to. In a story that doesn't dwell on a moral, we get more to think about, and we can shape the story in our minds to suit our needs. For example, I've gotten letters from readers of *Ella Enchanted* who've told me that the book made them more willing to obey their parents, because they realized that they, unlike Ella, had a choice. This is certainly a reasonable understanding to take from the book, but it wasn't a lesson I was pushing; it hadn't even occurred to me.

When I write, I don't think about a moral or a theme. I start with an idea or a question. In my book *The Wish*, for example, my question was, What would it be like for a character to get her wish to be the most popular kid in her school?

After I've written my book, sometimes I think about theme, which in this case is popularity, but I'm often at a loss to name a moral. In *The Wish*, things turn out for Wilma in a way that doesn't provide easy answers.

All my stories have themes, whether I give them no thought or hours of deliberation. Yours do too. Stories are always about something. The topics that engage you will bubble up whether or not you're concentrating on them.

Time to look at your old stories!

Pull out a few stories that you've worked on in the past. Ponder what the themes might be. There may be more than one in a story. See if the same themes reappear in story after story. It's okay if they do or don't. You may settle an issue for yourself in a single story and move on, or you may be working through something complicated.

More writing time!

- Use this moral in a story: "Think before you act." But don't necessarily prove the moral right. Your MCs are two friends, one who does think before acting and one who doesn't. They're both good people. Mix it up and make it complicated. Have acting without thought, possibly on instinct, work out well sometimes and not others. Don't decide which way your story should go—just make trouble and follow your characters.
- Expand my Otis example into a real story and bring in more characters. Don't decide until you get there what Otis is going to do about his failure.

Have fun, and save what you write!

·SECTION SIX·

Underpinnings

·CHAPTER 27·

Tense Choices

So far we've looked into the writing process, character, and plot. Let's move on to the underpinnings of storytelling. Charlotte wrote on the blog, "I've been thinking lately about tense, as in past or present. I've read some fantastic stuff in the present tense . . . and I've been wondering which tense a story should be written in, and how to decide."

I've chosen to write an entire narrative in present tense only twice, once in a novel and once in a short story. My historical fantasy *Ever* is in the present tense, and I wrote it that way because the survival of Kezi, one of my POV characters, is in doubt. I felt that if I used the past tense, readers would assume she's okay at the end. I also used present tense in a short story called "Little Time," which appeared in a book titled *Unexpected*. I used it in that case because my MC has to decide whether or not to shrink and join a society of long-lived tiny people. I wanted the reader right there with her as she chooses.

Otherwise, I've stuck with past tense, which generally seems more timeless and storybook-like to me than present. When we're deciding, we can ask ourselves which effect we want. We can also look at our old stories to see if we gravitate one way or the other, and then we can choose whether we want to go with our usual flow or if we want to write against it.

We can even incorporate both tenses into a story. Susan Cooper's novel *Victory* alternates between a modern narrator and a nineteenth-century one. The current-day chapters are written in the present tense, the historical ones in the past tense. I suppose they both could have been in one or the other, but this way works beautifully—and it's a terrific book.

Sometimes we won't have a strong reason to choose one tense over another. In those cases I'm prejudiced in favor of past tense, which I think is more flexible even when we're writing a gritty, contemporary tale. We can overcome the storybook feeling like this, for example: *Mickey spat cigar juice into the gutter and muttered, "You do that again, I'll knot your legs into a pretzel."* But it's harder to get that timeless aura in present tense. Let's take a medieval fantasy as an example, as in *Sir Grathnath turns to his liege lord and says,*

"I pledge my allegiance until the firmaments ripple and the seas grow trees." Then he dons his armor and buckles on his trusty sword. Doesn't sound right.

When I say I have a bias, I mean as a writer, not as a reader. As a reader I'm fine with either tense. If I like the story, I'm just happy. For a writer, though, present tense seems like more of a *decision*. Past tense seems more like, for good or ill, choosing the common path.

Flashbacks operate a little differently in each tense. If we're writing in present tense, we just have to switch to simple past. If we're already in past tense, we need past perfect with the auxiliary verb *had*, as I talked about in chapter 22.

When I was thinking about tense for the blog, I called Rosemary, my editor, to ask if she has a tense bias (I didn't tell her mine). She doesn't. She said the tense just needs to serve the story. I asked what kind of story is best served by which tense, and she thought that mystery and suspense stories sometimes benefit from present tense, allowing the reader to get inside the action. She also opined that present tense can be harder to pull off. She felt that flashbacks can be harder in present tense, the shift from present to past more jarring. She added that some authors try one tense, find it isn't working, and shift to the other.

I called Ginger, my literary agent, too, who had no preference either at first, but, after thinking a minute, said she might like present tense better. Then she became unsure again. We segued into a discussion of great beginnings. *Peter Pan*, for example, starts in present tense and shifts into past in midsentence. Here's how James M. Barrie does it (the underline is mine):

> *All children, except one, grow up. They soon know that they will grow up, and the way Wendy <u>knew</u> was this.*

See where the change happens? Like Barrie, we can switch to present tense even if we're writing in the past.

What we want to watch out for, though, is tense drift. Our story is steaming along in past tense when it suddenly shifts to present and then veers back. We don't do it on purpose for an important artistic reason; we simply fail to notice. It's not a big deal, just another thing to mop up in revision. When the story is finished, we want it to be consistent.

I've never read anything in the future tense, but it might be fascinating to try. The tense would lend an air of inevitability, as in *The passengers will mill on the dock, embracing friends and relatives. The Titanic's four smokestacks, straight and solid as anything made by man, will appear to be pillars supporting the sky*. Hmm.

Writing time!

- Rewrite the beginning few pages of one of your stories in the other tense—past if you're using present, present if you're using past. How do you feel about it? Which do you like better?
- Use these sentences as a story starter: *Nancy had seen this blue-headed boy before. It had been during school break in the fall, when she and her father had gone to the shore for one of their long rambles. They picked up knobby skipping tortoise shells and smooth driftwood.*
- Try writing a story in future tense. I suspect you'll need either a tragic ending or an upbeat one. A Roman myth might work well: a sad one, like the story of Pyramus and Thisbe, or a happy one, like the tale of Cupid and Psyche.

Have fun, and save what you write!

· CHAPTER 28 ·

Word Grazing

Possibly the most important appeal that ever came into the blog was posted by Maybeawriter: "I have a problem with my stories. I like the ideas, but the words never seem right. Please help!" And later she clarified with this: "Well, it seems like they don't flow right, or it seems like there is another word that might fit in better, but I can't really think of any, like there could be a better word for just walking, or the feel of the water."

Mark Twain wrote this: "The difference between the right word and the almost right word is the difference between lightning and a lightning bug."

Word choice influences everything. Going back again to M. T. Anderson's *The Astonishing Life of Octavian Nothing* (which astonished me in the best possible way), the reader is blessed with this sentence early in the book:

And so the answer to my perplexities, which must

appear in all its clarity to those who look from above, was finally clear to me: that I too was the subject of a zoological experiment.

Mr. Anderson's style, his voice in this book, perfectly represents my idea of eighteenth-century writing. Earlier, he describes the house where Octavian lives as "gaunt." I picture a narrow structure with long, skinny windows, painted gray, but not newly painted. When things get tough, Octavian becomes Observant. The term nails the character's experience. He distances himself from what's going on to merely watch, and it breaks my heart.

We improve our word choices by making friends with a thesaurus. The online thesaurus, www.thesaurus.com for one, often transports me beyond the words I usually use. And we learn about amazing, enormous English, which has tons, heaps, oodles, loads, scads of synonyms. For example, there happen to be a delightful array of words and expressions for *crazy*, like *bananas*, *batty*, *cracked*, *deranged*, *disturbed*, *dippy*, *dotty*, *flaky*, *flipped out*, *loco*, *loony*, *moonstruck*, *non compos mentis*, *nuts*, *off one's rocker*, *out to lunch*, *psycho*, *screwy*, *unbalanced*. I put some of these on the blog and people wrote in with more. Why so many? Are we all—listen for maniacal laughter—deep down *berserk*?

Then there are other words that have no synonyms, like poor lonely *stapler*.

Several kids posted on the blog about words that were banned in school, dubbed "jail" words by some teachers. Examples are: *good*, *bad*, *sad*, *mad*, *happy*, *grumpy*, *big*, *small*, *medium*, *love*, *nice*, *calm*.

I like all words, but I sympathize with teachers who want to develop their students' vocabularies. So wow your teachers with your fab vocab. Instead of *grumpy*, give them *irascible*, *peevish*, *querulous*, *vinegarish*. Use your thesaurus. It will help all your writing. For the heck of it, try for words your teachers will have to look up. They don't know every single word, either.

And in the stories you're not writing for school, forget about jail words and words that are allowed to run free. The dictionary and the thesaurus are your pastures. Graze at will on the weeds along with the grass and the flowers. Be a free-range writer.

Having said all this, there are kinds of words—parts of speech—to use sparingly, specifically adjectives and adverbs. Decide which of these two sentence sets you think is better: *I stepped back quickly. "Don't stab me with that long weapon!"* Or *I jumped back. "Don't stab me with that sword!"*

The second set, right? In the first sentence I changed *stepped back quickly* to *jumped back*, because it's impossible to jump slowly, so I no longer needed *quickly*. And in the second sentence I traded *long weapon* for *sword*, because our reader will know that a sword is long, and *long weapon*, which is vague, could be anything with a point. Nouns and verbs pack power. *Jump* is stronger than *step back*, and *sword* is stronger (and sharper!) than *long weapon*.

And take care with words that weaken, like *almost*, *slightly*, *somewhat*. Occasionally they're essential, but often they reflect an unwillingness to take a stand, as in *Hilda felt almost jealous*. Let's make her turn pea green with envy.

Sometimes we need adjectives and adverbs. There will be moments when we have to say a deed was done quickly or that something was long. We just want to give these words an extra going over to be sure they're needed.

I like to vary my sentence and paragraph beginnings. Two identical beginnings in a row are acceptable (my rule), but no more. However, I remember that no rule applies all the time. Sometimes repeating a beginning sets up a beat that I like.

My sentences tend to be short. That's how I write. That's my style. See? You may be different, and even I, when I remember, write against habit and merge two sentences with a *because* or *since* or *so*, because I like to shake things up, and you may too. Notice your sentence lengths and switch them up occasionally. Variety makes for a better read. If you reread this paragraph with attention to the sentences, you'll see a range of sentence lengths, from one word to thirty-five.

I change around my sentence structure, too. For example, I don't like sentence after sentence consisting of this happened comma and that happened. I also dislike a series of this-comma-but-that sentences, so I change *but* to *however*, *though*, *although*, or, better yet, recast the ideas entirely.

A critique buddy once remarked that I often use the verb *is*, which made me self-conscious and worried. I hadn't considered *is* before. *Is* isn't interesting, but it *is* unavoidable. However, now that my friend pointed out my frequent *is*ing, I've been rearranging some sentences to bring more striking verbs into the act. Still, whenever I read *is* in a sentence by an author I like, I think, See, even she or he does it. And Rosemary, my insightful and knowledgeable editor, whom you met in chapter 27, has chimed in to say that *is* is a disappearing word, meaning that the eye glides over it. It barely registers. Rosemary says it's okay to use and reuse. So that's settled.

Speaking of repeated words, in my first submission of *Writing Magic*, Rosemary found twenty zillion appearances of the word *stuff*. I hadn't noticed, maybe because I like the word, which feels friendly and informal—but I didn't like it enough to want it to show up seven times on every page.

I'm lucky to have editors who are sensitive to word

repetition, but I cultivate my own sensitivity too. Whenever I suspect that I'm overusing a word, I type it in a list above the title of my book. Just before I submit the manuscript, I do a document search on each word in the list. If a word appears too often, I consult the thesaurus for alternatives. You can adopt this method in your stories too.

On the other hand, in *Peter Pan*, James Barrie repeatedly uses the phrase "of course." I adore *Peter Pan* and think Barrie a supple stylist. When I wrote my books about the fairies of Neverland, one way I connected them to Barrie was by scattering "of course" with abandon.

On the other other hand, I once read that extraordinary words shouldn't appear more than once or twice in a whole book. For example, I like the word *susurration*, which means a whispering sound, because it's onomatopoeic (sounds like what it means). But I wouldn't use *susurration* more than once in a book. The reader would notice. The word would draw attention to itself and away from the story.

(Susurration is a noun without a commonly used verb form. Webster's dictionary shows no *susurrate*. Susurrate appears in the *Oxford English Dictionary* as rare. How interesting!)

If you want to play around with your own repetition, examine something short that you've written. Look for your tics—the words that crop up too often, your repeated sentence arrangements—and fiddle with them. As you continue to write your longer works, keep these habits in mind. I don't suggest you go back if you're in the middle of writing a novel. In fact, I think that would be a bad idea, not at all worth your time. When you finish and revise, however, look for your repetitions and ask your critique pals to look too.

No matter how carefully we pick our words, they're still a pale reflection of experience. We can never precisely write the feeling of water; not even Shakespeare could have. If we were writing to the man in the moon, who has never felt rain, we couldn't represent clearly enough the sensation of wetness. If the moon happened to drop out of the sky into a lake, and the man in the moon swam out, then he might say, "I get it now. Before I was just guessing."

Recently, some friends and I discussed the impossibility of describing the color red to someone who is blind from birth. We can talk about warm colors and cool colors, a red-hot metal, blood, a rose. We can describe the color wheel. A blind person will understand heat and blood and the idea of a color wheel, but he won't experience red. In *Fairest*, I invented the color htun, and I described it, but I've never seen it—wish I could. But I can come closer to picturing it than a blind person could because I already see colors.

Writing time!

- Pick a paragraph in a favorite book and rewrite it at least three ways using different word choices. Think about using bigger words or shorter words. Consult a thesaurus. You probably won't be able to change every word. Now see if you notice repeated sentence structures within the paragraph. If you do, recast them. Decide which way you like best. You may improve upon a master. Seriously!
- Describe water for the man in the moon. You won't succeed, but create a longing in him with your description, so that he can hardly bear not taking a bath or drinking. He's so desperate that he decides to visit Earth. Write a story about his time here.

Have fun, and save what you write!

·CHAPTER 29·

Clarity and Gizoxing

Along similar lines as Maybeawriter's post quoted in the previous chapter, Susan Lee asked, "Do you have any tips on writing? As in making sure people who read it will understand what you wrote?"

Unless you're creating experimental fiction, clarity is the primary objective, ahead of plot, characterization, setting—any of the elements of storytelling. Clarity isn't even an element! It's the air a reader breathes.

Being clear doesn't mean we can't be complex. We can suggest something that will be more fully explained later. Our reader doesn't have to understand what we intend at exactly the moment we suggest it. Realization can be delayed. Mysteries delay understanding constantly. That isn't lack of clarity, that's simply interesting storytelling.

But we don't want to confuse the reader accidentally, and we can do so by making technical mistakes.

For example, loose pronouns will muddle the reader. If I write, *The food was overcooked and everybody was arguing. It made me sick*, the reader doesn't know what *it* refers to—the meal or the arguing or both. *It* is the loose pronoun in this instance. And *sick* is imprecise, too, although it's not a pronoun. Heartsick or stomach sick? Explaining in later sentences helps, but being specific from the beginning is even better.

When two males or two females are together in a scene, clarity can be hard to achieve, as in *James waited an hour for Justin to show up. When Justin finally arrived, he was very angry.* This time the pronoun *he* is loose. Who was angry? James for having had to wait or Justin for some other reason? And yet *When Justin finally arrived, Justin was very angry* sounds terrible. What to do?

Recast it. *James waited an hour for Justin to show up.* New paragraph. *Justin entered the restaurant pale with anger. "If I ever have to wait another hour for my sister to finish practicing her flute, I'll . . ."* No confusion.

In *A Tale of Two Castles* the dragon character makes the pronoun business easier. Masteress Meenore is an IT because dragons rarely reveal their gender, so IT can be in a scene with a male character and a female character and, unless another dragon is present, confusion is impossible, and since IT is capitalized IT can't be confused with an inanimate object, like a bowl of soup or a shoe.

Finnish, I'm told, has no masculine and feminine pronouns. A man is an it and a woman is an it. I don't know if this creates a problem for people writing in Finnish, but I'm told it sometimes makes translation difficult.

The Elements of Style by William Strunk and E. B. White is a slim book about style and English usage. *Usage* means the way a word is used. For a guide to clear writing it can't be beat, in my opinion. A book that's devoted entirely to usage, like *Garner's Modern American Usage*, is helpful, too. Usage books are arranged alphabetically, dictionary style, a cinch to figure out.

The usage issue that gets me into trouble every time is the difference between *take* and *bring*. The examples that a usage book provides make me understand for at least five minutes. Other people often misuse *lay* and *lie*, a pet peeve of mine.

But usage changes, and if everybody keeps lousing up *lay* and *lie*, the rule will change and I'll have to get used (pun intended!) to it.

For those of you who are writing to have your work published, I suggest you take my advice about usage to heart. And here's a command about grammar and spelling: Get it right. An editor won't give the newbie writer any latitude on this. Only a rare editor will read beyond more than one misspelled word and even one grammatical error, like a mistake in agreement between noun and verb. Agreement means that a singular noun or pronoun requires a singular verb, and a plural noun or pronoun calls for a plural verb. This is the kind of sentence that sometimes gets people in trouble: *Either Mary or her little lamb is going to school* is correct, and *Either Mary or her little lamb are going to school* is wrong.

If you've finished a story, a novel, or a seven-book series that you want to submit to a contest or to a publisher and you're not certain that you've got all the pesky little elements right, ask an authority, like an English teacher or a librarian, to read your work. You can tell him that you don't want a critique of your plot or your characters, just the grammar, usage, and spelling.

Now enough of me as taskmaster! It is possible to write more or less understandably with nonsense words, and for word lovers like us, it's fun and a pleasant break from the hard parts of writing fiction. I made this up:

> *Marisette gizoxed down the previo at zyonga speed. If the ashymi didn't boosheg, she'd find herself and the precious kizage in the boiling svik and all would be owped.*

Boy, I hope that ashymi booshegs! We understand enough to grasp that otherwise Marisette is in deep trouble, whatever the trouble is. I don't know if we could keep this up through a whole story, but a little is a blast.

Along these lines there's Lewis Carroll's poem "Jabberwocky" in *Through the Looking Glass*, which is packed with action and words that have no meaning. Here are two stanzas:

He took his vorpal sword in hand:
Long time the manxome foe he sought—
So rested he by the Tumtum tree,
And stood awhile in thought.

And, as in uffish thought he stood,
The Jabberwock, with eyes of flame,
Came whiffling through the tulgey wood,
And burbled as it came!

Manxome sounds pretty bad and *uffish thought* in my opinion feels useless. Better stick with your *vorpal sword*, dude.

If you don't know the whole poem, I can't wait for you to read it. Try saying it aloud after you've read it to yourself a few times. Act it out. It's very dramatic.

When I read and reread the Lord of the Rings trilogy, I used to say the language of the orcs out loud because I loved the sound. Since then, I've made up fragments of several languages of my own, and you can too. Here are some of the questions I learned to ask myself:

- How will the language look? You have punctuation marks, capitals, and repeated letters or omitted letters to work with. Gnomic in *Ella Enchanted* and *Fairest*, for example, is punctuated backward and the capitals appear at the end of a name and at the end of the sentence. Abdegi, the language of the giants, also in *Ella Enchanted*, is missing the letters that have a soft sound, like the letter *f*.
- How will the language sound? Each of the languages in *Ella Enchanted* has a particular sound. Abdegi is accompanied by emotional noises, like whoops and howls. Every word in Ayorthaian begins with a vowel and ends with the same vowel.
- Will there be consistent meaning? When a word repeats in a language in *Ella Enchanted*, it's the same each time. I kept a glossary to make sure. For example, the Gnomic word *brzzay* always means "digging." By contrast, in *Ever* the word for digging might be *ioopll* the first time it shows up and *eressc* the next. My thinking was that Wadir, where the language is spoken, is a dreamlike place, and things shift unexpectedly in

a dream. If you decide to let meanings change, you should have a reason, as I had. Are you going to deal with grammar, tenses, plurals, etc., in your new language? I never have. I did a little with plurals and past tense in *Ella Enchanted* but not much, and I wasn't careful about it. However, more power to you if you go all out.

There's French (sort of) in *A Tale of Two Castles*—anglicized French, meaning that I gave French words an English spelling. One of the streets is Roo Street. In French, as you may know, *rue* means street. The ogre's name is Count Jonty Um, which comes from the French *gentilhomme*, and the meaning of his name has significance for the story, although it's okay if the reader doesn't get it; I would be crazy (bananas, batty, cracked, etc.) to require readers of a book in English to know French! To those who don't get it, his name is just Jonty Um, without any special significance. If you know another language to some degree (I don't speak fluent French), you can do what I did. I like putting inside jokes in my books that I can chuckle over, even if I'm the only one laughing.

When we fool around with languages we're exploring language itself, a worthy endeavor for a writer.

Writing time!

- Your main character seeks out another creature—could be a Martian or an elf or a dog or something else. Each needs something from the other, but they don't speak the same language. They may not even think the same way. Write their meeting and your MC's attempts to get what he wants. See if you can work the story around so they are able to figure each other out, but don't make it easy.
- Or, going the other way, your MC is the other creature, trying to communicate with a human.
- Invent your own nonsense words and put them in a paragraph or a poem. Max out on the made-up words while still letting the reader gain a sense of what's going on. If you try a poem, remember that rhyming is a snap with nonsense words. *Ashymi boosheg*, for example, can rhyme with *dusheemee goothegg*
- Write a romantic moment in which all the terms of endearment are incomprehensible, you adorable *quayth*.

Have fun, and save what you write!

· CHAPTER 30 ·

The Writing and Publishing Clock

Blog readers have expressed curiosity about my process and how my manuscripts become books. Here's a comment from Charlotte: "I was wondering if you could give us a breakdown on how long it takes you to write an average novel, from the inklings of an idea to the first draft to the printing to promotion, etc. What takes the longest? Do different books take significantly different amounts of time? Do you have deadlines?"

How long it takes me to write a book depends on the book. Some are easier than others. The longest was eight years for *Dave at Night*, but I didn't work on it regularly (I wrote *Ella Enchanted* in the middle). I spent the most continuous time on *Fairest*, because I couldn't get the point of view right. *Fairy Dust and the Quest for the Egg* took about nine months, quick for me. Most of my Princess Tales consumed only a few months, because they're shorter than my other novels; the quickest of them, *The Fairy's Mistake*, took an astonishing eight days! I was so happy! That one began life as a picture book, which was rejected by a zillion publishers. My editor for *Ella* liked it and asked me to turn it into a short novel and write two more—the start of the series. When I expanded it, I already had the story and knew exactly what I was doing.

I don't think the books that were the longest in the writing are the best or the worst, just the hardest. Some authors are much speedier than I am, and some are much slower. They're not better or worse writers; their processes are just different. Don't blame yourself for being fast or slow. The proof is in the pudding, not in how long it cooked. The reader doesn't know if we spent a decade laboring over a book or a fevered eight days. He can't tell if we revised a hundred times or if it went from our computers to the printer after an editor didn't change even a comma (Rosemary says this never happens).

If a writer misses a deadline, the book gets rolled over to the next season. My editor assures me this wouldn't ever be a problem, but I suspect otherwise. Editors move to other publishing houses (publishing companies are called "houses"). Publishers change direction. It's best to be on time if we can.

If you're writing against a deadline, when you're actually writing (not taking a shower or walking the dog), put the deadline out of your mind. It's a distraction. You're doing the work, which is hard enough without also worrying.

Revision deadlines can be tight, but I'm a revising warrior and I blast straight through. I'm known for meeting deadlines, which, I think, gives editors a nice comfort level.

But meeting any deadline comes second to making the story as good as you can make it, and often that can't be rushed.

On the publishing side, a novel takes about a year to a year and a half from when I submit a manuscript to Rosemary to its publication. I'm involved in some of what happens and have a rough idea of the rest, but I'm not an expert. For insight from an expert, you might like to read Harold Underdown's *The Complete Idiot's Guide to Publishing Children's Books*, which has it all.

Soon after I submit a manuscript, I start biting my nails. Will Rosemary like it? Often she phones or emails to reassure me, which is very kind. Then, after a few weeks, when she's had time to turn the book over and over in her mind, she sends me an editorial letter by email and by snail mail along with the manuscript, on which she's written her first round of edits. The letter always starts with what she liked and goes downhill from there, although she puts her criticism in the kindest possible light. My usual reaction is

Yikes! Can I fix it? This process, editorial letter and manuscript edits, is how Rosemary and I work together, but some editors do the initial work in a phone call or a meeting. An editor may not mark up the manuscript at this point; he may just suggest a direction the writer should take in the revision. I prefer receiving written edits. If Rosemary says my MC needs to be more likeable, for example, I need to see the places in the manuscript where she isn't or I won't understand.

Here is one difference between an editor at a publishing house and a teacher: when an editor gives you an edit, you're at liberty to make the change or not to. It's your book, and the final decision is up to you. Not so when your editor is your teacher.

Having said that, I take my edits very seriously. Rosemary and I have the same goal, to make the book better, and she has the advantage of objectivity, which I've lost by living and breathing my book day in and day out.

When I finish the revision, I email it back. After she goes through the new version, Rosemary sends me a blessedly shorter letter and her second edits. If things are looking pretty good after that round, she gives the manuscript to the copy editor, who looks for the nitty-gritty mistakes, like grammar, punctuation, and consistency. An example of consistency would be this: A character is twelve at the start of a book and two years pass, and when I mention his age again

I say he's fourteen. The copy editor would be looking out for this. If I said he was fifteen, she would catch it. We writers rely on the eagle eyes of copy editors! However, I still try to get the nitty-gritty right myself, and so should you. Mistakes are unavoidable, but too many make the manuscript seem sloppy, as if we weren't paying attention.

While all this is happening, more internal publishing action has begun, and the internal side continues until publication. First of all is the decision about when the book will come out. Publishers have seasonal "lists," meaning the group of books that will be released over the course of several months.

Deadlines are attached to the list decision. If I were late with a revision, the book might be pushed to the next list. Other things have to happen on time, too. For example, the cover art has to be commissioned and finished.

Back to me. Rosemary sends me the copyedited manuscript by email with e-edits in the margins. I e-write my responses and return them by email. If any questions remain, Rosemary emails me.

Galleys come next. They aren't a book yet, but the pages are designed as they will be in the book, and the typeface is what it will be, which is not up to me. It's chosen by the book designer, although Rosemary and the art director supervise. Once there are galleys, electronic editing is over. Changes are made on the physical page again.

The first version of the galleys is called the first pass. It's read by the proofreader, Rosemary, and me. By the time I get it, I see brief discussions among the others here and there in the margins. I love that. It's proof that getting a book right is important!

Everyone's changes are incorporated into second-pass galleys. The book is in good shape by now, but I look at second-pass galleys because I'm a chronic fiddler.

First-pass galleys are also bound, so that they look like a paperback book even if the real book will be released in hardcover, and even though they don't contain the final changes. A paperback is sent to me, not to work on, just to have, because this is the magic moment when I see my story as a book for the first time, and it never fails to be a thrill. I celebrate, dance around, and show it to my husband and to our Airedale, Reggie, who enjoys the jubilation.

The bound galley paperback is also mailed to reviewers and to important people in the world of children's literature who can help the book. It's sent out even though it still has mistakes, and readers are warned that some of the words may change.

Other things happen behind the scenes. A decision is made about the size of the print run (the number of books to be printed initially). Publicity and marketing plans are developed. The book is integrated into the programs that the publisher uses to market and promote every book. Editors present their books to the sales force, the people who will sell it to independent and chain bookstores and to online booksellers. Sometimes a book tour is organized.

Oh, and the book is printed! Then it's sent to distributors, who receive the orders and fill them. And it's turned into an ebook and made available in that form, too.

After all this, and more, on the publisher's side, it's a wonder that the process takes only about a year.

Writing time!

- Write from the point of view of a newbie author meeting his or her editor for the first time. Make it go marvelously well. If you haven't been published yet, make it a dream come true.
- Along the same lines, write a chapter or two in your future memoir about yourself as a writer, whether or not you expect writing to be your career. What got you started writing stories? Go into your real past, but also imagine the future. What has been a turning point or what will be? Describe your greatest past writing triumph (possibly a story or poem you're proud of or one that received praise) and your greatest upcoming one.

Have fun, and save what you write!

· SECTION SEVEN ·

Poetry Country

·CHAPTER 31·

Write Your Story a Poem

Here's the beginning of "How Do I Love Thee?" a poem Elizabeth Barrett Browning wrote to her husband, Robert Browning, who was also a poet:

How do I love thee? Let me count the ways.
I love thee to the depth and breadth and height
My soul can reach, when feeling out of sight
For the ends of being and ideal grace.

Obviously these are lines in a love poem from one person to another, but they express how I feel about poetry itself, which touches my heart and my mind just as profoundly as stories do. When I read or write poetry, I feel as if I'm extending invisible fingers into the center of my being and also out to the edge of the universe. It brings me joy to share this love with you.

Both poetry and fiction clasp writers and readers in an embrace of ideas and feelings. Both explore how it is to be alive, to struggle, to fail, to succeed, to remember, to imagine, to enjoy the natural world.

I've always been interested in both kinds of writing. When I was little, I wrote poems and stories, and my first publishing successes were with poems. Two were published in an anthology of poems by high school students. I have no recollection of what they said, and I wish I did, but, alas, back then I didn't save what I wrote.

As an adult, poems crept into my books for kids almost from the beginning. I wrote poems for *Ella Enchanted*, *Fairest*, *The Wish*, *The Two Princesses of Bamarre*, *Ever*, *Stolen Magic*, and *The Fairy's Return*. The poems in these novels crop up only occasionally, but my book *Forgive Me*, *I Meant to Do It* is a collection of funny poems. (Books of poems are called collections.)

For years I've gone to a January retreat that the writer Susan Campbell Bartoletti has organized for herself and other women who write books for children. Each retreat has been taught by a poet. I've come away from every one inspired.

Why? What do I need poetry for, when I'm primarily a writer of prose, and I earn my living from my stories, not my poems?

Do I *need* it, in addition to loving it? I think I do. Let's look at what poetry has done for some of my novels and what it can do for your novels and stories.

Early in *The Wish*, Wilma receives two love poems. Here's the first one she gets:

Wilma's sweet.
She's a treat.
Let's make a date.
We'll call it fate.
Boo hoo.
I love you.

This is the second:

My barking siren
My short-necked beauty
My long-toothed divine
Tie me to a tall mast
So I may not come at you
Stop my mouth with a silk bandanna
That I may not tell my hope
I think and dream and drink of you

Clearly, these two were not written by the same characters. So a poem can be an instrument of character development, and it works that way in most of my books that include poetry.

The first poem probably wasn't written by an original thinker. We can tell in just six lines. The second poem probably was. In eight lines we discover that he expresses himself well, that he's not afraid to show his feelings, and that he knows mythology.

This is an example of one of the main attributes of poetry: compression. Poems can squeeze a lot of ideas, emotions, and information into a few words.

Writing time!

Pick one of your stories, one you're working on now or one you already finished. Go into it and have two characters each write their own poem. The poem can be a love poem or a poem that reveals another feeling—anger, confusion, sorrow, joy—because poems are great at revealing feeling. It can rhyme or not rhyme. One of my examples does; the other doesn't. Take care to make the poem of each character reflect his or her personality.

Have fun, and save what you write!

In chapter 22 we talked about backstory. In *The Two Princesses of Bamarre*, fragments of an epic poem provide the backstory. The book begins with a stanza:

Out of a land laid waste
To a land untamed,

Monster ridden,
The lad Drualt led
A ruined, ragtag band.
In his arms, tenderly,
He carried Bruce,
The child king,
First ruler of Bamarre.

More fragments of the poem show up, and the reader learns the history of the kingdom and its great hero.

That's backstory, but a poem would also be a fine way of handling foreshadowing. A prophecy, for example, could be presented in a poem.

Fairest takes place in a kingdom of singers, and the songs, which are really poems, not only reveal character, but also move the story along. And they provide variety, which is one of the hallmarks of good writing. Poetry also adds liveliness and energy. A poem breaks up the stately progression of paragraph after paragraph of prose.

Writing time!

- In chapter 22 we looked at ways to present the backstory of Queenie (the Queen of Hearts). Let's have a poem do it. Hoping his wife will find some comfort, Kingie (the King of Hearts) has commissioned a poem to commemorate the assassination of Daddy Card, which will be read at the next anniversary of his death. You decide whether Kingie made a good decision or a bad one. Write the poem.

- Now let's use Queenie and a poem for foreshadowing. Seven of Diamonds, who is sick of the beheadings, plots against the royal couple, but Jack of Clubs is gifted with second sight. He wakes up one morning with a poem on his lips that hints at the plot, not precisely, but disturbingly. Write his poem.

Have fun, and save what you write!

·CHAPTER 32·

Write a Story in a Poem

We've seen how poems can contribute to a story, but we can also tell a complete tale in a poem. This kind of poem falls into a category called *narrative* poetry.

Below is a narrative poem I wrote that was published in *The Louisville Review*. Before you read it, you may need some background. Two elements of the poem come from Greek mythology. The first is Lethe, the river of forgetfulness in Hades, the mythic underworld. The second is Cassandra, a tragic figure. The god Apollo gave her the gift of prophecy, but when she angered him, he turned it around so that no one believed her whenever she accurately predicted the future.

Tarot cards are used by fortune-tellers. An acupuncturist, for those of you who don't know, practices a kind of Chinese medicine. The word *dolorous* means mournful, and *self-recrimination* is self-blame.

THE RIVER LETHE

The fourth graders crowd around
Cassandra's fortune-telling tent
at the state fair. A slender hand
opens the flap.
"Come in, children."

They file inside.
The tent's a fire hazard, lit by a dozen
candles, but Cassandra knows
it will never catch. Incense
smolders. Only Fletcher,
son of an acupuncturist,
recognizes the smell.

Cassandra sits behind a rickety table
that holds a crystal ball and a deck
of tarot cards. She's weeping.
They're so young.
"Who's first?" she asks.

"Me. Sara Allen."
Their teacher said to go alphabetically.
Sara is tall for her age, with a gap

between her two front teeth.
Cassandra keeps herself
from brushing the girl's long bangs away
from her eyes. "Don't marry the boy
with the ponytail. Remember."

"Will I have children?" Sara asks.
"Will I be a scientist?"

"If you remember. Next."

Grinning, Max Barshansky steps forward.
This is a game.

"July 20th, ten years from now, stay inside.
Lock your door. Remember."

The children come to her, one by one.
She tells them how to avoid tragedy,
ordinary misfortune, dissatisfaction,
disappointment, self-recrimination.

"Never go to Oklahoma."

"Everything does not depend on you."

"Eat your vegetables."

Gradually, her tears, her dolorous
Remember seeps into them.

They repeat her words. Murmurs
fill the tent.

The last child, Tyrone Williams, comes to her.
How straight he stands.

"Pick the navy if you must, not the army."

He nods. The navy. The navy.

The children leave
and blink in the bright sunlight.

A woman in overalls is spraying a bed of poppies.
The water runs in front of the tent
in a sparkling stream too wide to jump over.

The children step in somberly,
but by the middle they're stamping their feet
and laughing. Max shouts, "Look!
The roller coaster." They run toward it.

A sad story, right?

Here's where compression comes in: If we were to tell this in prose, we'd have to go on for much longer, and we'd need to be more obvious about the connection between the water the children walk through at the end and the river of forgetfulness.

We'd have to decide who our MCs are, maybe Tyrone Williams and Cassandra herself, or maybe Sara Allen and Max Barshansky, who, a few years later, ties his hair in a ponytail. Probably we'd extend the time in the tent, include side conversations, have the teacher poke his head in and get his own grim prophecy. This short poem could become a novel, as we spin out all these fates and discover if anyone escapes. We could go forward through the generations and turn this into a five-book saga.

But the story also stands alone as a poem.

There's a tradition of fairy tales and stories about fairies told in poems. Here's the haunting first stanza from "The Stolen Child," a poem by the famous late nineteenth century–early twentieth century poet William Butler Yeats:

Where dips the rocky highland
Of Sleuth Wood in the lake,
There lies a leafy island
Where flapping herons wake

The drowsy water-rats;
There we've hid our faery vats,
Full of berrys
And of reddest stolen cherries.
Come away, O human child!
To the waters and the wild
With a faery, hand in hand.
For the world's more full of weeping than you can
understand.

Haunting, isn't it?

Notice that long last line, which repeats at the end of every stanza. My guess is that Yeats made it that way for emphasis.

I've written a poem version of "Cinderella," which was published in an anthology of fairytale poems called *On the Dark Path: An Anthology of Fairy Tale Poetry*. This Cinderella is entirely different from my Ella in *Ella Enchanted*. In fact, I suspect Ella would have no patience with this one.

BECOMING CINDERELLA

Daddy admired the lady's lineage,
she his golden coins, so they married.

She embraced me, and I endured
the stoniness of her bosom.
Her daughters hugged me too, snatch
and release, heir faces turned away.

Daddy galloped off to fight in foreign wars.
If only my mommy had left me a hankie
with a magic teardrop to keep me safe.
My stepsisters stole my glass slippers,
my jewels, my nanny's care. They promised
to love me if I moved into a smaller room,
swept the fireplace, but not if I complained.

I became Cinderella, goo to their granite,
though they never loved me. The prince says
I needn't wash his hose or trim his toenails,
but I'm not taking the chance.

In addition to brief storytelling poems, entire novels have been written as narrative poems. You may have read some. This is the first stanza of the novel *Make Lemonade* by Virginia Euwer Wolff:

I am telling you this just the way it went
with all the details I remember as they were,

and including the parts I'm not sure about.
You know, where something happened
but you aren't convinced
you understood it?
Other people would maybe tell it different
but I was there.

Notice how readable this is, how relaxed the language. It doesn't get all stuffy just because it's a poem.

Soon, we're going to transform our own prose into poetry, but first, let's change where Jinny (Virginia Euwer Wolff is a friend) ends her first two lines:

I am telling you this just the
way it went with all the details I
remember as they were,

To me, this doesn't feel as pleasant to read. The new line endings don't seem as natural. For example, there's no comma after the word *went*, but when *went* is at the end of the line, we pause briefly. When it's in the middle, it zips right into the next word, and I wish for a comma to slow me down. Often, when we write poems we want a breath to come at the end of a line.

But not always. Poets sometimes end lines with *the*

because they want to pick up the pace; they want the reader to hurry to the next line. Maybe a surprise or an important idea is coming.

Stanza breaks introduce an even longer break than the end of a line. We can end a stanza at the end of a sentence. In "The River Lethe" each stanza does that. But they can also close with a comma or no punctuation at all. It's up to the poet.

Also, see that I incorporated dialogue into "The River Lethe." You can too.

Writing time!

- You've guessed that this was coming: Take a page from a story you're working on or from an old story and turn it into poetry. You'll be breaking your prose into lines, so consider your line endings, and think about when and how you want to move along to a new stanza, which may not always be at the end of a paragraph. Since we've looked at how poems are often more compressed than prose, see if you can find places to cut and simplify.

  Now, look it over. Try again, making different decisions about where to end your lines. Read your new version. Which seems more like a poem to you? If you're on a roll, fiddle with the lines some more. And, if you're enjoying yourself, continue, and turn the entire story into a long narrative poem.

- Write two fairy-tale poems, either from the same fairy tale or from different ones. Write one with a modern feel and the other with an old-fashioned feel, like we find in the Yeats poem. It's up to you whether they rhyme or not.

Have fun, and save what you write!

·CHAPTER 33·

Poetry Flies the Flag of Freedom

But not all poems are narrative, and not many find their way into novels. Probably the biggest reason I write poems is because I'm a word person. When we strip away story, what's left is words: the sound of them, the look of them, their meanings and double meanings, the ways we can arrange them on a page. Poets explore words in all their glory.

When I write a poem, my mind moves into another zone in my brain. Gravity isn't as strong here, time wobbles, and logic is out of kilter. The laws are looser than in fiction writing. Poetry flies the flag of freedom.

The nineteenth-century poet Emily Dickinson wrote, "If I feel physically as if the top of my head were taken off, I know *that* is poetry."

So she felt an amputation (temporary, I hope). I experience an addition, as if a ruby or an emerald is glowing inside my chest, and the glow fades slowly. After I write a poem—happy poem, sad poem, doesn't matter—I go around grinning smugly until that, too, gradually wears off.

This sad and angry poem that I wrote illustrates a few of the possibilities of poetry:

MARY SHERRI MARK DARLA JAKE NOAH OLIVIA

Why did *I*
go to the party

Mary Sherri Mark Darla Jake Noah Olivia
are feeding their faces

I

have a stomachache

Mary Sherri Mark Darla Jake Noah Olivia
are dancing

Mr. Stevens asks *me*
to dance

I

say, it's okay
and no

I

go to the bathroom
and stay there for half an H O U R

Outside I

hear Mary Sherri Mark Darla Jake Noah Olivia
laughinglaughinglaughinglaughing
their heads off

I

wish for their heads to

fall

off

More heads coming off, but not, I suspect, as Emily Dickinson meant! In this poem, the poet (me) regards the page almost the way a painter views a canvas. Words can go anywhere. I'm interested in the look of the poem as well as its meaning and feeling, although feeling predominates in this one. And the feeling is emphasized by the spacing of the words and letters, the crowding together of the happy party people, the isolated *I* and *me*, the capitalization and separation of the letters in the word *hour*, so we feel time ticking by, connecting the words in the laughinglaughing line.

Notice also the title of the poem, "Mary Sherri Mark Darla Jake Noah Olivia." Surprising, right? Poem titles have at least as much significance as book or story titles. In this case I'm emphasizing the crowd that the speaker of the poem feels excluded from. The first time I wrote it, I made the first word be the title and called the poem "Why." Poets do that sometimes, start the body of the poem in the title.

Punctuation is absent, but we know where to pause anyway, because of the line breaks and the occasional capitals. But you don't have to capitalize, either, if you decide the poem would be better served without it. E. E. Cummings, a famous twentieth-century poet, was known for putting words where he believed they should go, no matter what anyone else thought. He often made up words, used real words unconventionally, and ignored the rules of capitalization and punctuation. For example, occasionally he put a parenthesis in the middle of a word. The surprising title of one of his poems is "And What Were Roses. Perfume?For I Do." The lack of a space after the question mark isn't a typo; it's the way Cummings wrote it.

He and other poets sometimes fiddle with words themselves. Here are a few silly lines I made up to demonstrate:

The bab-
ooooooooooooooooooooooooooooooooooon
played for an our
with hour
ball-
oooooooooooooooooooooooooooooooooooon

Here I switched the words *our* and *hour*, and I broke the words *baboon* and *balloon* into two lines each and stretched out the *o*'s so you'd be extra aware of the *oo* sounds. I'm not claiming this is much of a poem or even a poem at all; it's just an example of the fooling around we can get into in poetry.

Three paragraphs ago, I wrote this about capitalizing: "But you don't have to capitalize, either, if you decide the poem would be better served without it." How do we make the decision about what's best for our poem?

We gain experience as we write more and more poems and read more and more poems, because it's as important for poets to read poetry as it is for novelists to read novels.

And just as we sometimes do in our stories, we try things more than one way. The brevity of poems makes experimentation less time-consuming than in stories. We can move words around, change capitals and punctuation, try a new title, and have a revision in just a few minutes. We can rework the poem again and again, and then compare versions to see which we prefer.

Poets expect more from the reader than fiction writers do. When we write stories, we make entry as easy as possible, because we want the reader to lose herself in our plot. But most poems are too short to get lost in. Instead, we want the reader to regard a poem in much the same way as people look at a painting. With a painting, we have a response: we like it or we don't or we want to think it over; we notice the colors, the paint texture, the composition, the size of the canvas, the way it makes us feel. With a poem, we have a response: we like it or we don't or we want to think it over; we notice the placement of the words, the rhyme or lack of rhyme, the meaning (which may be clear or not), the length, the way it makes us feel. We may linger over a poem, just as we stand for several minutes in front of a painting, or we may turn the page.

Writing time!

- Write a poem about one of the seasons, or about an event, like the first day of school, using your words, lines, punctuation, and capitalizing in the unexpected ways we've just discussed.

- Rewrite your poem three ways, making new decisions about the look of the poem. Decide which you like better. Put the poems aside for three days and then reread them. Has your favorite changed? Revise again, if you discover ways to improve one or all of them.
- Write an argument poem, but instead of using quotation marks, put the different voices on different sides of the page. If you like, you can move the voices closer together when they agree, farther apart when they disagree.
- Write a poem about an activity—playing basketball, cooking, walking the dog, whatever—and make the placement of the words, along with the meaning, show what's going on.

Have fun, and save what you write!

·CHAPTER 34·

Rhyme Time

So far, except for the Yeats stanza in chapter 32 and one of the poems from *The Wish*, the examples I've given haven't rhymed. Whether or not to rhyme is another decision the poet gets to make, and there is no right or wrong way to go. A poem is bona fide poetry whether or not it rhymes.

When I do see rhyme or hear it, a pleasurable *buzz* runs through me, a little *zzzt!* Almost any kind of rhyme does it, sometimes with the added fillip of thinking, *Aren't I clever?* for noticing.

I say *almost any kind of rhyme* because there are quite a few. There's the kind we all know, called *end rhyme*, obviously because it comes at the end of the line.

Excuse me, but this little narrative poem from my childhood pops up in my mind. Maybe you know it too:

OOEY GOOEY

Ooey Gooey was a worm,
a mighty worm was he,
standing on the railroad tracks,
the train he failed to see . . .

. . . Oooooeey! Gooooeey!

He and *see* are end rhymes. But there's another kind of rhyme in the first and last line of this charming jingle. *Ooey Gooey* is an example of internal rhyme, because it happens inside the lines, not at the ends.

Here are two more examples of internal rhyme, these from the Yeats stanza. I've underlined the words I want you to look at:

To the waters and the wild
With a faery, hand in hand.
For the world's more full of weeping than you can
understand.

Than and *can* are separated by the word *you*, but that's okay. The rhyme still counts. Above them, *and* and *hand* are in different lines, but it's still internal rhyme. A few lines could divide them, and the rhyme would still be legit. *Understand* and *hand* are end rhymes, but they also rhyme internally with *and* and with *hand* inside the line.

Aside from being internal, these rhymes—*than* with *can*, *and* with *hand*, and *Ooey* with *Gooey*—are just like the end rhyme example, *he* with *see*, in that they rhyme exactly. In sound they're the same except for the beginning of the word. Such exact rhymes are called *perfect*.

If you're stuck for a rhyme, a rhyming dictionary is the place to go. I find mine online, and sometimes I consult more than one. But don't depend entirely on dictionaries. Often your brain will send you more creative rhymes than the dictionaries offer.

Here's a bit of a ditty that excited and horrified me when I was little, which also features worms. The versions I found online are different, but this is what I used to sing in a quivering voice:

The worms crawl in,
the worms crawl out.
They chew your guts
and they spit them out.

Poor starving worms, never swallowing! The rhyme comes from the repetition of the word *out*. When a word rhymes with itself, it's called *identical rhyme*. There are a lot of technical terms in poetry!

Another kind of rhyme is called *slant rhyme*, and it may be my favorite. It's almost rhyme, like *stink* with *skunk*. I underlined two slant-rhyming words in this poem by nineteenth-century American poet Emily Dickinson:

> *"Hope" is the thing with feathers—*
> *That perches in the soul—*
> *And sings the tune without the words—*
> *And never stops—at all—*
>
> *And sweetest—in the Gale—is heard—*
> *And sore must be the storm—*
> *That could abash the little Bird*
> *That kept so many warm—*
>
> *I've heard it in the chillest land—*
> *And on the strangest Sea—*
> *Yet, never, in Extremity,*
> *It asked a crumb—of Me.*

Soul and *all* both end in an *l* although the vowels are different. That's the kind of rhyme that makes me feel clever when I notice it. (*Storm* and *warm* also have different vowels, but the sound is the same, at least in my New York accent, so I'd count this rhyme as perfect.) If you're writing a rhyming poem and you can't come up with an exact rhyme that fits your poem, you can broaden your thinking to include slant rhymes. To help you out, most online rhyming dictionaries offer a slant- or near-rhyme option.

The only sort of rhyme I'm not fond of is forced rhyme. I'll show you what I mean by example:

Jill did frown
when Jack fell down.

In ordinary speech we'd never say, "My best friend Jill did frown when I yelled at her." The word *did* is present only to *force* a rhyme.

Here's another example:

She gave him the globe full of snow
just out of friendship, not for show.

A snow globe isn't even filled with real snow; I just put it that way so it would rhyme with *show*, because it's much harder to find a perfect rhyme for *globe*—I might have to pull in an *earlobe*!

Poets of long ago often forced the rhyme. That was okay back then and not a flaw, but today's poets prefer more natural phrasing.

Forced rhyme can be great in a funny poem, however. Here's one by twentieth-century poet Ogden Nash, known for his *light verse*, which means humorous poetry:

THE DOG

The truth I do not stretch or shove
When I state that the dog is full of love.
I've also found, by actual test,
A wet dog is the lovingest.

Most of us, if we've spent time with a dog, have experienced being used as its towel!

The first line in Nash's poem is twisted around so that it ends with *shove*. In ordinary speech we'd say, *I do not stretch the truth*, but Nash wanted to end with *shove*, an unnecessary, *forced* word, to get to the rhyme. And *lovingest* isn't a word we usually come across. But what fun it is! And how satisfying those silly rhymes are.

Still, aside from light verse, poets of today usually go for more conversational wording. Let's try the Jack and Jill example like this:

Jill frowned
when Jack fell down.

Frowned is an absolutely completely acceptable rhyme for *down*. The ear barely registers the *ed*.

Let's take another example:

Sorceress Annie did break
the bad news to Wizard Jake.

Replace *did break* with *broke* and we get a fine slant rhyme with *Jake*. If the rhythm seems wrong, we can add a word or two like this:

Sorceress Annie sighed and broke
the bad news to Wizard Jake.

Perfectly natural, right?

Slant rhyme examples like *soul* and *all* are also called *consonant rhyme*, because the final consonants are the same, but not the vowels. (*Broke* and *Jake* above are also consonant rhymes, since the final *e* is silent.)

If there's consonant rhyme, naturally there must be *vowel rhyme*, also known as *assonance*. An example would be *elf* and *pen* because of the short *e*.

There are more kinds of rhyme, a surprising abundance. I won't name them all, just a few more: *apocopated* (I love the sound of this word, pronounced uh-POCK-uh-payted, which sounds to me like popcorn popping), in which a syllable is missing, as in *stinker* with *clink*; *mosaic* rhyme, where a single word is rhymed with more than one, like *assail* with *a snail*; and *eye rhyme*, when the sounds aren't the same, but the letters are, as in *bone* and *gone* or *dough* and *cough*.

In my favorite kind of rhymed poem, the rhyming is so subtle and natural that I don't even see it at first. A contemporary poet who's great at rhyme is Molly Peacock. Here's a beautiful poem by her:

THE THRONE

When I was afraid, fear took me in,
and gave me a cold seat in her kingdom
from which I looked for all my kin
and found no mother, no father. Dumb

I was, and deaf then. Touch only I had,
only the cold claws of the chair arms did
I feel, and hollowness in my head.
My mother was dead. My father was dead.
I gripped the throne of fear with my right hand,
and the seat of the chair held me upright
or I would have fallen. I couldn't stand.
But the throne's left arm was warm with human might.
It took my hand and held me in its own,
that the kingdom of fear might be overthrown.

Look at these end rhymes: *kingdom* with *dumb*, *had* with *did*, and *in its own* with *overthrown*. And notice the internal rhyme in the twelfth line: *arm* with *warm*. The whole poem is thrilling, and the rhyme adds to the excitement.

And here, for pure delight, is a rhyming poem by the nineteenth-century English poet Edward Lear. When you come to it, don't let *runcible* stop you. It's a nonsense word Lear invented.

HOW PLEASANT TO KNOW MR. LEAR

How pleasant to know Mr. Lear,
Who has written such volumes of stuff.

Some think him ill-tempered and queer,
But a few find him pleasant enough.

His mind is concrete and fastidious,
His nose is remarkably big;
His visage is more or less hideous,
His beard it resembles a wig.

He has ears, and two eyes, and ten fingers,
(Leastways if you reckon two thumbs);
He used to be one of the singers,
But now he is one of the dumbs.

He sits in a beautiful parlour,
With hundreds of books on the wall;
He drinks a great deal of marsala,
But never gets tipsy at all.

He has many friends, laymen and clerical,
Old Foss is the name of his cat;
His body is perfectly spherical,
He weareth a runcible hat.

When he walks in waterproof white,
The children run after him so!

Calling out, "He's gone out in his night-
Gown, that crazy old Englishman, oh!"

He weeps by the side of the ocean,
He weeps on the top of the hill;
He purchases pancakes and lotion,
And chocolate shrimps from the mill.

He reads, but he does not speak, Spanish,
He cannot abide ginger beer;
Ere the days of his pilgrimage vanish,
How pleasant to know Mr. Lear!

Writing time!

- Pick a poem you've written and look through it for rhymes you didn't know were there. Underline them. Look for synonyms you can switch in to add more internal rhyme. If you find any forced rhyming, reword with any of the kinds of rhymes we've discussed (consonant, vowel, mosaic, apocopated, identical, and eye).
- Try a *bouts-rimés* (from French, pronounced BOO ree MAY), which requires at least two people. Each person writes a list of rhymed words, like *joke*, *flop*, *smoke*, *drop*, *inhale*, *plate*, *derail*, *great*. The participants exchange lists

and each has to write a poem using those end rhymes. When you get your list, be wild. Poetry doesn't have to be logical.

- Use my words for a rhymed poem: *joke*, *flop*, *smoke*, *drop*, *inhale*, *plate*, *derail*, *great* (or *grate*). Don't worry about meaning. If you're able to cobble together something that makes sense, fine, but go for the pleasure of the sounds.
- Write a rhymed poem about yourself or about someone you know. If your creation turns out to be light verse (as Edward Lear's is), you can force the rhyme to make it funnier.

Have fun, and save what you write!

· CHAPTER 35 ·

Playing with the Poetry Deck

In poetry, words, syllables, and letters are like playing cards. Form poems are the games you can play with them. With cards, we have gin rummy and poker and go fish and many more. In poetry we have forms you know or have heard of, like the haiku, acrostic, *bouts-rimés*, and sonnet. And there are others you may or may not know, like the pantoum, tritina, triolet, and villanelle.

Poetry can be divided into form poems, which are guided by rules, and free verse, which flies that flag of freedom—unrhymed, with no regular rhythm, no required number of lines, no set repetition, no prescribed approach. I enjoy the openness of free verse, and I relish coloring inside the lines of form poetry. I'm willing to lower my flag for the effects I get with form poems.

In support of form poems, I have to confess that sometimes when I finish writing a free verse poem, I'm not sure I've really written a poem or just a paragraph that I broke into lines. I'm not even always sure about the free verse poems I read in books and magazines. With those, I figure they must be poems because a publisher published them!

But form poems are more likely to feel poem-y to me, so let's try a form poem called a *persona poem*, which is a poem written in someone else's voice. This should be familiar territory, because we do it all the time when we write fiction from a first-person POV.

I once wrote a persona poem in the voice of Jughead from the *Archie* comics. You've already read my Cinderella persona poem, and I've also written fairy tale poems in the voices of Rapunzel and the youngest dancing princess from "The Twelve Dancing Princesses."

Here's the beginning of a persona poem that I wrote from a dog's POV, which appeared in an anthology called *The Poetry Friday Anthology*:

YOU MISBEHAVE

Dear Human,

When you came home today, you let me lick you
and you scratched me behind the ears

for just two minutes before you left
for soccer practice with your real friends.
Then, later, you ate fried chicken and scraped
the bones into the trash where good dogs don't go,
and you filled my bowl with Fido's Friend,
which tastes like mold.

You get the idea. So let's start writing time with one or more persona poems. My poem happens to be in the form of a letter, which makes it also an *epistolary poem*, but yours doesn't have to be. If you're writing from the persona of someone you know, make the poem sound as much like that person as you can. For example, if he says "Listen!" often, work the word into the poem once or twice. If your persona is a historical figure, imagine how that individual might express herself. Don't rhyme unless your persona would speak in rhyme. Along those lines, it might be fun to write a persona poem with Dr. Seuss as the persona.

Write a poem in the voice of one or more of these:

- A friend or someone in your family or a teacher. You don't have to be nice. If you're not nice, however, or if you're downright mean, keep the poem to yourself or read it (softly) to your cat.
- An animal, as I did. Could be your cat. Since cats and other animals don't usually speak, this poem can rhyme.

- An inanimate object, maybe something that has a history. Or not—could be the sandwich you're about to eat. This poem, too, can rhyme.
- A historical figure or a celebrity.
- A character in one of your stories.
- A character you love in a book, a movie, or a fairy tale.

A delightful aspect of persona poems is that you can reveal secrets. Suppose you're writing in the persona of the Loch Ness monster; you can tell what it feels like to be him (or her or it). Or the poem can take place in a phone booth, and Clark Kent can report his thoughts as he becomes Superman.

Now let's try another kind of form poem, this one called a triolet (pronounced TREE-uh-lay). It's from France, which I bet you already guessed. One of the charms of the triolet is that we have to write only five lines to get an eight-line poem, because two of the lines repeat. I made up this example, which has just a few words so you can see what's going on pretty easily:

STOLEN

Ancient book,
magic spell.
Don't look.

Ancient book
I took.
Don't tell.
Ancient book,
magic spell.

Notice that the first, fourth, and seventh lines are the same, and so are the second and eighth lines. The triolet rhymes, too: the first, third, and fifth lines rhyme; and the second and sixth lines rhyme. Naturally, the repeated lines rhyme with themselves (identical rhyme, as you may remember).

This is a longer, scary triolet I wrote:

BAD DAY

When I enter the tall, tilting house on the hill
my hands make fists. I wish it weren't Halloween,
wish the silence didn't stiffen with ill will.
When I enter the tall, tilting house on the hill
I hear a voice. "At last, a guest. Welcome, Bill,
brave Bill, who won't live to turn fifteen."
When I enter the tall, tilting house on the hill
my hands make fists. I wish it weren't Halloween.

When you write your own triolet, you may find it helpful

to follow the method I use: As soon as I wrote the first two lines in "Bad Day," I copied them into the places where they would repeat, like this:

BAD DAY

When I enter the tall, tilting house on the hill
my hands make fists. I wish it weren't Halloween,
[new line]
When I enter the tall, tilting house on the hill
[new line]
[new line]
When I enter the tall, tilting house on the hill
my hands make fists. I wish it weren't Halloween.

That helped me see what was coming up. I did one more thing, too:

BAD DAY

When I enter the tall, tilting house on the hill
my hands make fists. I wish it weren't Halloween,
[new line ?ill]
When I enter the tall, tilting house on the hill
[new line ?ill]

[new line ?een]
When I enter the tall, tilting house on the hill
my hands make fists. I wish it weren't Halloween.

The question marks followed by letters remind me of the rhymes I need to end the line with.

Let's look at my silly poem again:

STOLEN

Ancient book,
magic spell.
Don't look.
Ancient book
I took.
Don't tell.
Ancient book,
magic spell.

Notice that *book* is followed by a comma the first and last time it appears but not the second time. You don't have to preserve the punctuation in the repeated lines, and the capitals can change, too.

In my examples, the lines are all about the same length,

but that's not a requirement of a triolet. You can decide to use short and long lines.

Sometimes eight lines (three of them repeated) are too few to express what you want to say. You can keep going and pile one triolet on top of another. Here's a double triolet by the contemporary poet Dana Gioia:

THE COUNTRY WIFE

She makes her way through the dark trees
Down to the lake to be alone.
Following their voices on the breeze,
She makes her way. Through the dark trees
The distant stars are all she sees.
They cannot light the way she's gone.
She makes her way through the dark trees
Down to the lake to be alone.

The night reflected on the lake,
The fire of stars changed into water.
She cannot see the winds that break
The night reflected on the lake
But knows they motion for her sake.
These are the choices they have brought her:

The night reflected on the lake,
The fire of stars changed into water.

Beautiful, isn't it? Solemn, too, right?

Now that you've appreciated the poem, notice the dramatic change in punctuation in the second appearance of the first line in the first stanza. Here it is the first time:

She makes her way through the dark trees

and here's the second:

She makes her way. Through the dark trees

Writing time!

You've been expecting this: Write your own triolet or more than one. These are some topics you can try, or pick your own:

- A storm.
- A haunted house, as I did, but imagine it your way.
- Feelings before or after a big event.
- Thoughts about someone remembered but no longer in your life.

Have fun, and save what you write!

· CHAPTER 36 ·

Come Again?

The pantoum (rhymes with *tan room*) is another poem form that uses line repetition. Even more than the triolet, the pantoum calls for planning. Writing one is like playing a strategy game; we always have to look ahead. When I'm working on a pantoum, I feel as if my brain cells are shooting off sparks—in a good way.

Notice how the lines repeat in this pantoum of mine:

DEPARTURE

Farewell.
You just arrived.
I must leave.
Where are you going?

You just arrived.
I have an appointment.

Where are you going?
The cliffs above the sea.

I have an appointment
with a sage who roams
the cliffs above the sea.
He speaks the language of lizards.

With a sage who roams,
I have become a wanderer too.
He speaks the language of lizards
to bring truth to reptiles.

I have become a wanderer too.
I must leave
to bring truth to reptiles.
Farewell.

Let's go through it with the lines numbered. The left column shows the lines in order. The next column shows the repeats.

DEPARTURE

1	*1*	*Farewell.*
2	2	*You just arrived.*

3	3	*I must leave.*
4	4	*Where are you going?*
5	2	*You just arrived.*
6	6	*I have an appointment.*
7	4	*Where are you going?*
8	8	*The cliffs above the sea.*
9	6	*I have an appointment*
10	10	*with a sage who roams*
11	8	*the cliffs above the sea.*
12	12	*He speaks the language of lizards.*
13	10	*With a sage who roams,*
14	14	*I have become a wanderer too.*
15	12	*He speaks the language of lizards*
16	16	*to bring truth to reptiles.*
17	14	*I have become a wanderer too.*
18	3	*I must leave*
19	16	*to bring truth to reptiles.*
20	1	*Farewell.*

As you can see, the second and fourth lines of every stanza return as the first and third lines of the next. The last stanza has a twist in the way it repeats the first and third line of the first stanza, which so far are the only lines that haven't repeated. The third line returns as the second line of the last stanza, and the first line becomes the final line of the poem, so the poem starts and ends with the same line, like a poetry sandwich.

We can rhyme a pantoum or we don't have to. We can write as many stanzas as we like, but the reader won't get the full effect without at least three. Below is another unrhymed pantoum I wrote:

HOODLUM ROBIN

He stole from the poor to make himself rich,
that horrible hoodlum Robin. Maid Marion,
who faithfully believed in his honor,
said, "Robin, I trust you no matter what."

That horrible hoodlum! Robin made Marion
his girl with a gold ring. "Dearly beloved,"
said Robin. "I trust you no matter what."
She kissed him and wore the glittering gift,

his girl with a gold ring. Dearly beloved
Marion swore to change his thieving ways.

She kissed him and wore the glittering gift,
the only penniless person he ever gave to.

Marion swore to change his thieving ways.
Who faithfully believed in his honor?
The only penniless person he ever gave to!
He stole from the poor to make himself rich.

Although the words in the lines repeat exactly, the punctuation and capitalization often change. Quotation marks come and go, and one of the words shows up as *maid* the first time it appears and *made* the next. Did you catch that? The second line of the poem reads like this:

that horrible hoodlum Robin. Maid Marion,

In the next stanza it's this way:

That horrible hoodlum! Robin made Marion

I haven't broken any rules. It's fun to fool around with words in a pantoum.

Some poets, including me, occasionally change a word here and there in a line or two. Some poets change many words, and some keep the repetition only in the last word of the line. I'm more of a traditionalist, but you can try any way of doing it. If you're pleased, that's good enough.

Pantoums can explore or express an idea or tell a story. If we decide to tell a story, often the line repetition will take us in surprising and fascinating directions. We just have to remember that we're going to need to circle back at the end to the lines from our first stanza. Sometimes that circling back requires more stanzas than we expect.

Here's the same tip as I gave with the triolet: Drop down and fill in the repeat lines to come. This is what I did. Right after I wrote the first stanza of "Departure," it looked like this:

Farewell.
You just arrived.
I must leave.
Where are you going?

You just arrived.
[new line]
Where are you going?
[new line]

I didn't know how many stanzas I was going to wind up with, so I put just one more in:

[new line]
[new line]
[new line]
[new line]

Then I typed in what I knew of the last stanza.

[new line]
I must leave
[new line]
Farewell.

It's easier to write a pantoum when each line is its own complete sentence, but we get more variety if our sentences sometimes snake into the next line. When you write yours, try it both ways.

Writing time!

Write your own pantoum, or write a few. Make yours at least three stanzas long, although more are even better.

When I teach pantoums, I have the students work on their first pantoum in pairs. You can do the same. If you want to, write your first with a friend or a family member. Then try a few on your own.

If you like, you can use a couple (no more!) of my lines to

get you started. For example, you can move these two lines from my first poem into yours:

Where are you going?
The cliffs above the sea.

Or you can take any other two lines from either poem, and you can change my punctuation. It's not stealing as long as you give me credit. Poets borrow other poets' lines all the time. I won't mind as long as you do this:

YOUR TITLE
—after Gail Carson Levine's "Departure"

Or you can pluck a line or two from any poem, even from Shakespeare—and give him credit, too!

You can write a pantoum about anything, but if you're at a loss for ideas, here are some suggestions:

- A tall tale.
- An argument.
- Your pet.
- An emotion.

Have fun, and save what you write!

·CHAPTER 37·

Listen!

Remember my poem "Mary Sherri Mark Darla Jake Noah Olivia," with the words placed unexpectedly? Here's the end of the poem:

Outside *I*

hear Mary Sherri Mark Darla Jake Noah Olivia
laughinglaughinglaughinglaughing
their heads off

I

wish for their heads to

fall

off

We get the full effect only by seeing the poem, unless I could come up with a special way of reading it, jumping around or pointing as I spoke.

But many poems are written for the ear as much as for the eye. Poets give "readings," because poetry is meant to be heard. It's a personal art, possibly the most personal form of writing, and to hear a poet reading her own work, to hear her breath—maybe her voice catches at a particular moment—to hear her pause, swallow, is a special thrill.

So read your poems aloud. When you do, you'll join an ancient tradition, which almost certainly started even before writing began. Poems were easier to remember than tales told in prose because of the rhymes and the rhythm or the repetition of sounds or words. We find repetition in prose, too, but in prose we often cut our repeated words, as we discussed in chapter 28. In poetry we repeat on purpose although we choose our repetitions carefully.

I mentioned vowel rhyme or assonance before, the recurrence of a vowel sound, but I haven't mentioned alliteration, although you may know the term. It's the repetition of the same sound at the beginning of a word. (Not the repetition of the same letter, necessarily. *Cheese crackers*, for example, doesn't alliterate.) Remember the tongue twister *Peter Piper picked a peck of pickled peppers*? That's alliteration on steroids!

Let's look at a few examples from my pantoum about Robin Hood. You'll see that I've emphasized the alliteration. Here are the first three stanzas:

He stole from the poor to make himself rich,
that horrible hoodlum *Robin.* Maid Marion,
who faithfully believed in his honor,
said, "Robin, I trust you no matter what."

That horrible hoodlum*! Robin* made Marion
his girl *with a* gold *ring. "Dearly beloved,"*
said Robin. "I trust you no matter what."
She kissed him and wore the glittering gift,

his girl *with a* gold *ring. Dearly beloved*
Marion swore to change his thieving ways.
She kissed him and wore the glittering gift,
the only penniless person *he ever gave to.*

The alliterative words don't have to be right next to each other, but they should be in the same neighborhood, or we'll miss the effect.

Alliteration helps us remember a phrase. It's catchy! We may recall Marion's name down the centuries because it's usually coupled with "maid," and the *m* sounds fix it in our minds.

We find alliteration in prose, too. We see it in brands, like Dunkin' Donuts, Krispy Kreme, Coca-Cola. And in book titles, like Shakespeare's *Love's Labour's Lost* or Tolkien's *The Two Towers*, and, ahem, my *Ella Enchanted*. You can use it, too.

Coming up is an example of a particular kind of repetition, called *anaphora*, which means repetition at the beginning of a line or stanza. This excerpt is from a very long poem called *Jubilate Agno*, written by the eighteenth-century poet Christopher Smart when he was confined in an insane asylum with only his cat Jeoffrey for company. Read this aloud too. Here it is:

For he can fetch and carry, which is patience in employment.
For he can jump over a stick, which is patience upon proof positive.
For he can spraggle upon waggle at the word of command.
For he can jump from an eminence into his master's bosom.
For he can catch the cork and toss it again.
For he is hated by the hypocrite and miser.

Modern poets generally break up the anaphora a bit to add interest. In addition to the anaphora in these lines, notice the alliteration. For example, there's *patience* and *proof* and *positive*. What other alliteration do you see?

And did you catch the internal rhyme of *spraggle* (a word I can't find in the dictionary but that I can picture) and *waggle*?

You may know this one:

THE TYGER

by William Blake

Tyger! Tyger! burning bright
In the forests of the night,
What immortal hand or eye
Could frame thy fearful symmetry?

In what distant deeps or skies
Burnt the fire of thine eyes?
On what wings dare he aspire?
What the hand dare seize the fire?

And what shoulder, and what art,
Could twist the sinews of thy heart?
And when thy heart began to beat,
What dread hand? and what dread feet?

What the hammer? what the chain,
In what furnace was thy brain?
What the anvil? what dread grasp
Dare its deadly terrors clasp!

When the stars threw down their spears,
And watered heaven with their tears,
Did he smile his work to see?
Did he who made the Lamb make thee?

Tyger! Tyger! burning bright
In the forests of the night,
What immortal hand or eye
Dare frame thy fearful symmetry?

I wish tigers could hear this and discover how at least one human admired them!

William Blake asks lots of questions. A word that repeats often is *what.* So does *thy*, adding to the poem's majesty.

Writing time! Write a poem:

- with these assonances: long *o* and long *a* (not in every word, of course—but work them in as often as you can). These sounds linger, so try for a lingering mood, which might be eerie or sad or mysterious;

- with anaphora, in which several of the lines start with one of these words or phrases: *I wish, actually, when, do not, long ago*;
- with as much alliteration as you can work in. Some topics might be:
    - an event you're looking forward to;
    - an event you're dreading;
    - an adventure your pet might have if the world were a little different;
    - the day an elf visited you;
- that repeats at least four of these words: *bell*, *camera*, *haunting*, *hero*, *apple*, *halo*, *cloud*, *dream*, *echo*, *mermaid*, *flight*, *shine*.

Have fun, and save what you write!

·CHAPTER 38·

M. E.

The initials above don't stand for ME, but for *metaphor* and *endings*. The poets of this world would throw me in jail if I left M. and E. out.

Let's start with metaphor. Not every poem needs a metaphor, but many have one or two. It's an important way to help our poems feel poetic. Metaphor means the imaginative substitution of one thing for another. Broadly used, metaphor includes simile, which is when we expressly say one thing is like another. Here's Shakespeare using metaphor in *Romeo and Juliet*:

> *But soft, what light through yonder window breaks?*
> *It is the east, and Juliet is the sun.*
> *Arise, fair sun, and kill the envious moon,*
> *Who is already sick and pale with grief*
> *That thou, her maid, art far more fair than she.*

Not only does Shakespeare turn Juliet metaphorically into the sun, he gives the moon an illness, another metaphorical move, which turns this into an *extended metaphor*, one that carries through an entire poem or a big portion of it.

Let's look at the metaphors we've already met. In my poem "The River Lethe," the water that runs outside Cassandra's tent substitutes for the river of forgetfulness—a metaphor.

And take this line from my poem "Becoming Cinderella":

I became Cinderella, goo to their granite

She isn't really goo; they're not granite. It's a metaphor. I wasn't thinking, *I should toss in a metaphor now.* It just crept in. Yours will too.

Emily Dickinson's poem that starts, " 'Hope' is the thing with feathers" is an extended metaphor, because hope isn't actually a bird. But the metaphor is apt, isn't it? Hope defies gravity, as birds do, and at improbable moments it sings and won't be silenced.

Let's take another look at the first two lines of Molly Peacock's "The Throne":

When I was afraid, fear took me in,
and gave me a cold seat in her kingdom

There's no real kingdom, no actual throne. It's an extended metaphor!

And how about these lines from "The Tyger":

When the stars threw down their spears
And watered heaven with their tears,

I'm not sure exactly what Blake means, but I think the lines are gorgeous. No extended metaphor here, just metaphors.

Writing time!

- You may know the expression "sick as a dog." But certainly a dog isn't the only possibility when it comes to illness; dogs aren't always sick. Think of something else to be sick as, like, sick as a whale that swallowed a submarine. Jot down a few possibilities.

  Complete these other simile beginnings with unexpected endings:

  - hopeful as
  - watchful as
  - excited as
  - suspicious as
  - bored as
  - angry as
  - thrilled as

Use three of these, or three others that you come up with, in a poem.

- Let's dare to imitate Shakespeare with an extended metaphor poem. Turn someone you know or one of your characters into an object or an animal. Start the poem with the words *I call you*. Could be *the basket*, *the shoe*, *the hammer*, *the camel*, or anything else. As you go along, think of ways this person is like the metaphorical thing. For example, the person who is the basket may collect stuff. She may yield surprises; you dip into her and never know what you're going to get; she may wear clothes with colors that remind you of the muted colors of many baskets. In your poem don't mention those aspects of her that have nothing to do with a basket.
- This prompt was suggested by a book about writing poetry, *The Poet's Companion* by Kim Addonizio and Dorianne Laux. Call your poem an emotion, like Anger, Grief, Joy, or Impatience. Now write the poem without mentioning the title, but make the reader experience the feeling.

Have fun, and save what you write!

On to E., endings.

Stories end when the problem they present is resolved,

either happily or unhappily. Narrative poems may end the same way. Let's look at the ending of "Ooey Gooey" again:

the train he failed to see . . .

. . . Ooooeey! Goooeey!

A tragedy, and that worm is history!

The ending of a pantoum is settled as soon as the poet decides on the first line. Here's the first and last stanza of my pantoum, "Departure":

Farewell.
You just arrived.
I must leave.
Where are you going?

I have become a wanderer too.
I must leave
to bring truth to reptiles.
Farewell.

We've closed a circle, and the poem feels complete.

But usually poets have to search for the endings of their

poems, and the end needs to belong uniquely to the poem. What we want most of all is for the reader to feel content that the poem has come to rest.

Here are the first three lines of Ogden Nash's "The Dog" again:

The truth I do not stretch or shove
When I state that the dog is full of love.
I've also found, by actual test,

If we didn't know that final line, we might expect a mushy, sentimental ending, possibly *Of any breed, my Spot is best.* But the last line isn't that at all:

A wet dog is the lovingest.

It's a surprising change of direction, a great way to end a poem. In fact, there's a name (naturally) for this kind of thing, either at the end of a poem or in the body of it. It's called the *poetic turn*. At a poetry reading, when a poem ends in a turn, a surprise, one often hears a sigh run through the audience.

Molly Peacock's poem "The Throne" ends with a turn, when the arm of the cold throne becomes warm and supportive.

Here's the ending again of "How Pleasant to Know Mr. Lear":

He reads, but he does not speak, Spanish,
He cannot abide ginger beer;
Ere the days of his pilgrimage vanish,
How pleasant to know Mr. Lear!

This charming poem ends on a semiserious note with a hint of his death someday. Death is certainly one way to get completion! Seriously, though, mortality is a time-honored subject of poetry.

The sound of the words can make a poem feel complete. If you end with a line full of alliteration or assonance, or if you bring in a rhyme at the end of an unrhymed poem, your reader is likely to feel satisfied.

Writing time!

- Look over the poems you've written. Pick one that could use some strengthening at the end. Search for synonyms that will enhance the alliteration or the assonance in your poem. If it's not a rhyming poem, work in a final word that rhymes with the ending of a line not very far above.
- Write your own surprising poem about a pet.

- Write a poem about a season or a period in your life and end with movement to a new time.

I've come to the end of the poetry section, except for a final poem. This is a poem I adore, which celebrates writing. It's about writing poetry, but I think it covers every kind of writing.

WRITING IN THE DARK

by Denise Levertov

It's not difficult.
Anyway, it's necessary.

Wait until morning, and you'll forget.
And who knows if morning will come.

Fumble for the light,
and you'll be
stark awake, but the vision
will be fading, slipping
out of reach.

You must have paper at hand,
a felt-tip pen, ballpoints don't always flow,

pencil points tend to break. There's nothing
shameful in that much prudence: those are our tools.

Never mind about crossing your t's, dotting your i's—
but take care not to cover
one word with the next. Practice will reveal
how one hand instinctively comes to the aid of the other
to keep each line
clear of the next.

Keep writing in the dark:
a record of the night, or
words that pulled you from the depths of unknowing,
words that flew through your mind, strange birds
crying their urgency with human voices,

or opened
as flowers of a tree that blooms
only once in a lifetime:

words that may have the power
to make the sun rise again.

· SECTION EIGHT ·

Closing the Circle

·CHAPTER 39·

On Blogging

Returning to where we began, with the blog, reader Leslie Marie wrote, "How about a post about WRITING blogs? I'd like to start one but have absolutely no idea what to write. I think my biggest block is just fear of some sort holding me back!"

My blog is just my blog, a universe of one. To educate myself a little about the wider blog world, I checked out the blogs of a few fellow writers for children and young adults. Some wrote about themselves and their lives, which you can do too: chronicle your days and provide insights into the person you are. A friend suggested that I do the same, which in a way would be making myself into a character, because we can never present our entire personalities in all our complexity; we have to decide which aspects of ourselves we want to share. I imagine this kind of blog as similar to writing a memoir. The memoirist becomes a character, someone whose company the reader enjoys.

This sort of blog would also be somewhat like journaling, if you were journaling for more than yourself. Suppose you visit your Aunt Susan and you blog about the day. Well, you want to give your reader an image of your aunt, so you write that you adore her. You say she wears her brown hair pulled back in a ponytail, and her lipstick is always fading. *Is there a brand that sells faint lipstick?* you wonder. (You can post photos of her, too, if she gives you the okay.) When you hug her tight, you're surprised at how thin she is under her big wool sweater.

This is great stuff because it's full of detail, and we should put as much detail into our blog as we do into our fiction. Blogging is writing, after all.

Then Aunt Susan starts questioning you about the month since you saw her last. She's such an amazing listener that you remember occurrences you had almost forgotten, and, because she's so sympathetic, you confess something that had embarrassed you, a little event. She declares it of no consequence, which makes you feel utterly relieved. You post all this on the blog, too, minus the embarrassing incident. You're no longer ashamed of it, but you still don't want a stranger coming across it while doing an internet search—because we have to remember always that when we click *publish* on our blog, we're doing exactly that. A blog is a form of e-publishing. Our blog is going out to anyone in the *entire world* who has web access.

Suppose the afternoon with Aunt Susan proceeds happily until she asks about your best friend, Nora. The two of you quarreled last week and you absolutely don't want to talk about that. Even though you tell her you don't want to discuss it, she says, "All the more reason to get it off your chest," and suddenly you wish you'd never come.

This last part we shouldn't post. While we must be aware and concerned that strangers can see our blog, the likelihood is much greater that people who love us will read it, which includes Aunt Susan, whose feelings would be hurt. If we want to let her know her badgering is unwelcome, we should do so privately.

Suppose the afternoon continues downhill, and our thoughts turn downright hostile. In your journal, to be read only by you, you might write those angry thoughts. You might let yourself be whiny and resentful. You might wonder why you're cursed with such a nosy aunt, and why she has to heat her house to ninety degrees, and why she can't cook anything other than meatloaf, which tastes like shredded cardboard. That's fine in a private journal. Ranting is one of the joys of journaling. But not in a blog. These things follow us for decades!

(An advantage of fiction is that we can make one character whiny and another nosy, and no one will identify the character as us and our real-life Aunt Susan.)

Now that I've scared you silly, I'd like to say that blogging is very worth doing if you're careful.

In addition to writing about your life in general, you can:

- Pick a single aspect of your life to blog about, like public or private school or homeschool or babysitting or your writing (again exercising caution about negative remarks or—*important!*—the slightest hint that might be taken as threatening).
- Take a journalistic approach and report on any trips you take or on local doings, such as fairs, museum exhibits, concerts.
- Blog about world, national, or local news and present your own perspective.
- Have friends write guest posts.
- Present interviews with interesting people in your life.
- Blog about subjects that interest you. For example, you could review books.
- Write a how-to: how to make pie crust from scratch, how to paint with watercolors, etc.
- Create a visual blog with your photos and drawings.

- Offer information that people may need or want.
- Combine all the above. While I've made my blog about just one thing, yours doesn't have to be.

As an example of the next-to-last kind of blog on my list, Agnes, who follows my blog and who is homeschooled, created her own blog as a resource for homeschoolers. It's a wonderful idea. I'd guess there are lots of homeschooled kids and their parents who welcome the information, and curious people, like me, who were educated in classrooms.

Like Agnes, I chose to blog about a subject I know well, and my blog is a how-to about writing. I'm very aware of my blog readers out there in cyberspace, so I set a tone that I hope is friendly, encouraging, down-to-earth, and funny. The blog does create a version of me as a character. In real life, I possess the qualities I show there—but of course I'm more complicated, and I have my bad moments, too.

I aim for clarity and usefulness. I want readers to be able to put my posts to work. If I'm ever less than clear, I like being told, and if people have follow-up questions, I welcome them.

I don't know what I would have done if blog readers hadn't started asking questions. I could have written about what I was grappling with week-to-week in my writing, but I wouldn't have thought of all the topics they've raised. So

I'm grateful. When someone comments a few times, I start to feel that I know her, that I have a new writing pal in the ether of the internet.

Then there's the frequency of your blog to consider. If you're interested in collecting an audience, you don't want to disappoint them by dropping out of sight for six weeks. Some people post daily, some weekly, and some when the fancy strikes—but I don't think bloggers in the last group are concentrating on readers. I post weekly, every Wednesday.

And there's length. Some who post every day deliver short bursts. Others write long daily posts; I don't know how they find the time. My posts are substantial. I'm not satisfied until I fill two single-spaced pages and start a third.

For those of you who'd like to attract an audience to your blog, there are strategies you can use. I searched online for "how to bring traffic to a blog" and found a bunch of sites. You can too. To start, however, you can tell everyone you know about your blog and ask them to spread the word if they like it. The way I started to build an audience was entirely accidental. I was invited to write a message for NaNoWriMo. In it I included the URL for my blog, which was pretty new. My message went live, and—boom!—I had followers. Whenever I speak at a school or a conference, I say how to find my blog and website. The numbers continue to build, but slowly. I would love it if readers of this book come for a visit. You'll find some topics that I haven't gotten to here and some new posts. I gave the URL in chapter 1, but here it is again:

www.gailcarsonlevine.blogspot.com.

If you get a readership, be polite! If someone asks a question, answer it. If you receive a compliment, say "Thank you." Readers will likely be drawn in and come back for more.

Occasionally, someone may *flame*—that is, comment unpleasantly, even outright nastily—or may post something inappropriate, as happened once when someone wrote in with a product ad. You have the power to delete, so use it! You're responsible for the content and tone of your blog, which means you should check it regularly.

I also looked online for "blogs about writing," and found lists of the most popular sites, which have many more subscribers than I do. I'm sure my blog is also visited by people who never sign up. The other blogs must have such visitors too. The most popular bloggers guest post on other blogs and include guest posts on theirs. They also host book giveaways.

It seems that people can earn money by blogging, which I do not do—except when reading my blog causes someone to buy one of my books. Some sites carry advertisements.

If a reader clicks, the blogger gets paid (but very little per click). One of the blogs I saw had a tab through which a visitor could hire him as a freelance blogger or writer. For any of you who are thinking about ways to be a writer and earn a living while you establish your place in literature, blogging may be part of the picture, but you'll have to do more research. Social media keep changing. We need to stay up-to-date.

I end every blog post with prompts, many of which are in this book. A nonwriting blog wouldn't include prompts, but a how-to blog might end with an activity. In case you're planning a blog about writing or are just curious, this is how I make up prompts: I mull over the topic I've been discussing, like plot or character development or, in this case, blogging. I wonder what's in it that I can use. A blog-writing prompt would be good. Hmm . . . Where can I find conflict? Aunt Susan! Maybe Nora, too. And the possibility of trouble from exposing oneself unguardedly online.

Here goes. Writing time!

- Whether or not you actually set up an online blog, write a post for three different kinds of blogs.
- Write a story about your MC Madison and her aunt Susan. Create an argument. Resolve it happily or not. Bring best friend Nora into the story.

- Madison blogs about the confrontation with Aunt Susan. She's careful not to write anything that will hurt anyone, or so she thinks, but Nora sees the post and reads between the lines when her name comes up. Write Madison's post and what follows from Nora. Again, resolve it happily, or not.
- Madison applies to a music school (or starship school or unicorn-training school) she desperately wants to get into. Her audition goes brilliantly well, or so she thinks until the school rejects her. She's furious and posts her rage on the blog, suggesting that the school's admission policies are rigged. Write how this post changes her life.

Have fun, and save what you write!

We've reached the happy ending, but—oops!—I failed to mention that the best part of blogging has been the conversation with other writers. I cherish that, and I've loved extending the discussion in this book.

I doubt if we'll ever use up all the possible writing topics, because we writers poke our pens (and computers) into every aspect of living: the problems, the suffering, the oddities, the joys. We keep asking, What next? And what after that? We explore it all, and so the conversation never runs out, writer to writer.

INDEX